We Build People

Making Disciples *for the* 21st Century

Michael H. Clarensau, Sylvia Lee, Steven R. Mills

foreword by **George O. Wood**

Developed by the

Sunday School Promotion & Training Department

GOSPEL PUBLISHING HOUSE
Springfield, MO 65802-1894
02-0698

Library of Congress Catalog Card Number 96-075948

International Standard Book Number 0-88243-698-8

Printed in the United States of America

Contents

Foreword

When our children were small we taught them not to say, "I'm going to church." Rather, we wanted them to say, "I am going to where the church meets."

The church is not a physical building. We are the building of God (1 Corinthians 3:9).

Later, in our children's teenage years, I pastored a church during a major relocation and construction of new facilities. I put so much energy into the physical plant and the fund raising necessary to build it that the Holy Spirit reminded me I had gotten things out of focus. Midway through the building project, I dreamed one night that it was dedication day. The new building was up. The place was filled with people. I stood at the pulpit joining the assembly in praise to God with raised hands. At that moment in the dream I felt the Lord say to me: "So, the building is built—but, more importantly, did you let Me build you during this process?"

I awoke and realized that my priority on the external building was misplaced. My first attention needed to be on the construction the Lord wanted done in my own life and in the flock of God He had called me to.

I needed to be reminded that *we build people.*

For the past several years, Assemblies of God churches in America have reported in excess of 300,000 converts annually. However, less than 100,000 persons are baptized. Could it be that over two-thirds of those who say the sinner's prayer check out of the very next step in discipleship?

Our Sunday school and Sunday morning worship services also do not reflect an annual gain of 300,000. Our growth in these areas has been minimal in recent times.

What's happening?

Could it be that we need to become more effective and intentional at building people and diligent regarding Jesus' command, "Make disciples . . . teaching them to obey everything I have commanded you" (Matthew 28:19,20)?

This book, *We Build People,* is a practical resource tool for our churches to enfold persons into the body of Christ, then motivate, equip, and release them for ministry to others.

It lays out a practical four-step program for building people:

Base 1—Include Them
Base 2—Instruct Them
Base 3—Involve Them
Base 4—Invest Them

Not every Christian has an "edifice complex"! *Edify* originally meant "to build a house." Paul became concerned over some in the Corinthian church who were focused only on their own need to "shine" rather than on the upbuilding (edification) of the whole Body. He encouraged the entire church to have an edifice complex (1 Corinthians 14:12).

Ultimately, of course, it is the Lord who builds His church (Matthew 16:18). In that edifice He is the Chief Cornerstone, and the apostles and prophets who wrote the Scriptures are the foundation (Ephesians 2:20). We are the "living stones" He is using to build a spiritual house (1 Peter 2:5). The Holy Spirit invites us to be part of the construction process by building up ourselves in the faith (Jude 20) and building up others also (1 Thessalonians 5:11).

We are told to be careful how we build (1 Corinthians 3:10). Why? Because all of us, as Christians, are building something. And one day our construction will be tested to determine whether or not we built well (Matthew 7:24–27; 1 Corinthians 3:12–15).

Perhaps you have been busy building a career, a nest egg, a skill, a house. All these goals are, in proper context, commendable. But our chief goal should be to build that which will last for all eternity. People are the only part of this world that is eternal. Therefore, we must take special care that we do more than labor on those things that are temporary.

As you study and incorporate the material in this book into your life, you will find yourself becoming eternally productive in your walk with the Lord and service to His people. Christ's cause will be furthered as you too become involved in the greatest construction project of all: the building of people!

—George O. Wood
General Secretary of the General Council of the Assemblies of God

1
The Individual and Discipleship

Every human being is intended to have a character of his own; to be what no others are, and to do what no other can do.
—William Ellery Channing[1]

People. They come in all shapes and sizes. No two are just alike. As the pinnacle of God's creation, each possesses his or her own unique desires, attitudes, and abilities. Indeed, if variety is the spice of life, there are few things spicier than a room full of people.

The marketing genius of modern advertising has captured this uniqueness. One hamburger restaurant promised to let you "have it your way," while a well-known hot dog producer guaranteed satisfaction to every size and shape and type of kid, "even kids with chicken pox!" A manufacturer will produce a product in a dozen different varieties hoping to capture the fancy of individual taste. Personal preference can be exercised in everything from cosmetics to automobiles. Every shelf proclaims the message of individuality, making the priority of the individual a multimillion dollar creed.

Advertising giants aren't alone in their focus. Virtually every aspect of modern culture and modern thought is consumed with individuality. Legislation that secures the rights of the individual above all else is now most common. Judicial rulings increasingly use the same standard as their ultimate aim. The needs, desires, hopes, and dreams of the individual have become the centerpiece of modern society.

What about the church? On any given Sunday the sanctuary is peppered with new faces. Each comes from his or her own unique background and faces his or her own set of unique challenges. Each comes seeking the solutions to a wide variety of needs. For most, the church's ability to address those individual needs will determine issues of future attendance and involvement.

Is the church for the individual? At first, the question may seem ludicrous and unnecessary. After all, encountering God is a personal experience, and relationship with the Eternal One is extended to each person. Yet, a close look may reveal the validity of such an inquiry. In the church, focus can often shift to congregational needs, program performance, class sizes, or people groups. Teachers teach classes. Specialists target baby boomers or other societal groups. Evangelists call for winning entire schools or communities for Christ. What about the individual? Could it be that the church no longer views people as individuals, but just as a part of various groups?

Scott is a new college graduate. At 22, he is single, starting a new job in a new community, and excited about his future.

Jackie is a single mom who daily wrestles with the joys and challenges of her two teenage boys.

The Kellys hadn't been to church as a family in nearly six years. Last Sunday, Mom and Dad brought all five children into the crowded sanctuary.

To what group do these new friends belong? Will their first few encounters with a local congregation provide individual attention or seem like a relatively ordered mob scene?

Unfortunately many Scotts and Jackies slip through unnoticed and unaffected by a local church. Families like the Kellys will make the enormous effort to get five children cleaned and pressed for church only so many times before they wonder if anyone cares. Left to fend for themselves among the dozens of other worshipers, the Kellys will soon seek out new ideas or agendas for giving their lives meaning.

A well-known investment company claims that it "measures success one investor at a time." For the church, where the investments are eternal, that message must be even stronger.

Discipleship and the Individual

One of the most important decisions in any organization is to know "what business you're in." A company that produces a product must know that product is its business and that the product must remain its primary focus. When attention drifts to side issues or products, the effectiveness of the organization deteriorates.

A restaurant is in the food business. While one restaurant may construct the most comfortable dining room in town or use the most attractive napkins, that restaurant cannot afford to forget that its primary business is producing quality meals. No one will ever see the beautiful napkins or enjoy the plush accommodations of the dining room if the quality of the food has not remained the focus. Napkins are a side issue. The restaurant is in the food business.

What business is the church in? Is it in the building construction business? How about the travel and tourism business? No, the church is in the people business. Although many things happen in the life of a church, the central mission of the church focuses on people. The church's primary business is to introduce, guide, and train people for an eternal relationship with God.

A church may build buildings to accomplish its primary business, but its primary business is to build people. Scott and Jackie and the Kellys with their five children are the church's priority, not its music or its facilities. Just as the restaurant will be judged by the caliber of its food, so the effectiveness of the church must be judged by its impact in the life of each individual.

If the building of people is the measuring stick of a church's effectiveness, then how are we doing? George Barna, in his book *Today's Pastors,* looks at this question in detail. Consider the following observations adapted from his book:[2]

1. Many regular attendees are not truly Christian in the biblical sense. A majority of the people who attend Christian churches are not Christian, even those who have been attending the same church for nearly a decade.
2. Regular attendees are ignorant of basic tenets of faith. Lay members, despite fairly regular attendance by about half of the population, remain largely ignorant of the basic tenets of faith and are at best moderately committed to building a community of believers who are devoted to serving Christ with passion, urgency, and abandon. From their perspective, churches are only moderately helpful in dealing with life, and they perceive the influence of the Christian church on the decline.

Add to Barna's insights about the spiritual condition of many church members the following statistics from a national survey conducted by the Church of God:[3]

- 60 percent of all Americans attend church at least once per month
- 12 percent of Americans read their Bible
- 25 percent of church members admit they never pray
- 35 percent never read their Bible
- 60 percent never give to missions
- 70 percent never assume responsibilities in the church
- 85 percent never invite anyone to church
- 95 percent never win anyone to Christ

If the church's primary business is to build people, these numbers indicate that the church is struggling in its mission. In George Barna's research, church leaders listed the top priorities of their churches as follows:

1. Motivating people to pursue spiritual growth
2. Motivating the laity to engage in ministry

3. Increasing involvement by the laity in evangelism
4. Improving the training and equipping of the laity
5. Developing significant relationships with nonbelievers[4]

In spite of these priorities, the statistics listed earlier do not reveal overwhelming success. In an era where worship attendance has shown a steady increase, the effectiveness of the church in its effort to build people seems headed in the opposite direction.

What must we do to change this trend? The local church must ask the following: "What of eternal significance happens in the life of each individual while in the care of our church?"

Such a question propels us to the realization that in the ministry of the church, the building and developing of the individual must be central. The first and foremost of the local church's values must be that *every individual is valued and is the focus of our ministry.*

Scripture and the Individual

While there are many models and potential structures for ministry, the principle of the individual must become nonnegotiable. Church history has proven that culture and sociological trends may impact the program or style of the church, but the requirement that individual life-change be central is a timeless absolute.

Nowhere is the priority of the individual more vivid than in the life and teaching of Christ. He established a pattern both for His disciples and for His church today. That pattern focuses clearly on the needs of and ministry to the individual. Jesus revealed that true discipleship or building people is personal, pervasive, and primary.

Building People Is Personal

Understanding the ministry of Christ includes accepting a near paradoxical view of the individual. Peter reports Jesus' clear statement that His Father's goal was that *none* perish, but *all* come to repentance (2 Peter 3:9). That's everybody—a good-sized crowd by any measure. Jesus revealed that both He and the Father were motivated to see the salvation of the over 20 billion people who have lived in creation's history. That huge crowd doesn't even include those who are yet to be born.

Jesus also tells us that the incredible agenda of salvation for every person will never exceed the rate of one individual at a time. Salvation is never a group experience. In Revelation 3:20 Jesus' familiar words state, "'If anyone hears my voice and opens the door, I will come in and eat with him, and he with me.'"

The individual nature of God's plan overwhelmed the psalmist David. Psalm 8 reveals his wonder, "When I consider your heavens, the work of your fingers, the moon and the stars, which you have set in place, what is man that you are mindful of him?" (vv. 3,4).

Why does God, who formed the massive universe, so intently focus on the individual? The question may be beyond an answer. But since He has prioritized the individual, how can we not? That question must be addressed.

Jesus' teaching communicates the centrality of the individual, but His life made this even clearer. The compelling story of Zacchaeus, the diminutive tax collector singled out by Jesus is one remarkable evidence (Luke 19). John's record of the encounter with the Samaritan woman at the well gives further proof of His focus on individuals (John 4).

Another such proof was the deliverance of the Gadarene demoniac (Mark 5:1–20). He had been abandoned among the tombs, conveniently forgotten by his generation, but not by Jesus!

Jesus even canceled a burial procession to give a mother back her son (Luke 7:11–17). Bartimaeus' unique need for sight was met by the Savior who then helped him deal effectively with criticism (Mark 10:46–52). Children were a priority to Jesus despite the attitudes of those who held them back

(Mark 10:13). Even a thief was important enough for Jesus' attention, though the intensity of His own suffering was enormous (Luke 23:40–43).

If there is any further doubt as to Jesus' priority on the individual, it must be laid to rest by His description of a shepherd. "'Does he not leave the ninety-nine in the open country and go after the lost sheep until he finds it?'" (Luke 15:4). Can there be a clearer statement of the value Christ places on each individual?

A survey of the entire Bible reveals that God always prioritized the individual. From Hagar to Rahab and from Lot to Habakkuk, God's love singled out each individual. This marvelous desire for the individual gave strength to Gideon and Samson and gave hope to Abraham and Hosea. Even the bright light on the Damascus road was intended for just one set of eyes.

The Scriptures give even more evidence of God's value on the individual. Repeatedly we see that not only is God's love extended to the individual, but His power is displayed through individuals. Often people today find strength in the crowd. After all, it is easier to push a stalled car with ten men than with two. Having a hundred people on one's side gives a feeling of strength that a group of eight can't provide.

We call this group mentality "strength in numbers." It's this principle that makes us so fond of crowds. But the kingdom of God is not dependent on such a principle. The biblical text reveals that one is enough for every challenge if empowered by God. For conquering Goliath, one stone from the sling of one shepherd boy proved sufficient. One Samson, full of the power of God, was more than enough challenge for an army of Philistines. Even the single lunch of a lone little boy provided a banquet for thousands.

Why focus on the individual? Because in the economy of God's kingdom, the priority of one and the power of one serve as centerpiece.

TRUE DISCIPLESHIP IS PERVASIVE

Crowds celebrate uniformity. People tend to cluster around their physical similarities or shared ideologies. Individuals often will even lay aside those things that make them unique in order to melt into the masses around them. Inclusion in the "right" or "in" crowd becomes the goal. Those left on the outside of the crowd are cast aside as less than important. The crowd dictates the agenda. The crowd rules.

The Bible celebrates uniqueness. The limitless creativity of the Creator proclaims that individuality glorifies the Master. God's crowd requires only one. Therefore, no one is left on the periphery. There can be no outcasts if the focus is the individual. No one is left out of a group of one.

The biblical account seems to take pleasure in the pervasive nature of God's love. No individual is beyond His reach. This marvelous truth of God's focus on individuals is evident in many of the Bible's stories. The woman caught in the act of adultery is a clear example (John 8:1–11). The crowd had predetermined her fate according to the law. She was beyond hope because of the nature of her sin. Death by stoning would end this final day of her life.

In this great account of Christ's individual care, He established that even this sinful woman was not beyond His love. Her guilt was never in question. Her ultimate forgiveness and new life give proof that every individual matters.

The thief crucified next to Jesus is yet another proof that guilt of even heinous crime does not prohibit an individual from being led into God's care. The only crowd that had included this guilty man now sat on a Roman death row. But the thief, as an individual, desperately needed a Savior, and he found one in a most unlikely place.

While the love of God can reach even the most wicked sinner, the quest is for the outcast as well. In fact, several Scripture passages indicate that the outcast is not only welcomed but intentionally sought and targeted. Jesus proclaimed that His primary goal was to bring good news to the poor (Luke 4:18). He championed the needs of the oppressed. Indeed, throughout the Old Testament God placed great priority on loving the unlovable.

What is the meaning for us of God's focus on the individual's need? It is too easy to isolate individuals or groups who do not fit the ideal. Ministries built for the attractive ignore the unattractive. Ministries designed for the financially stable alienate the needy. Wherever ministry is designed for the group, someone is on the outside.

Every individual, regardless of behavioral background, social status, or personal charisma, is valued and must be the focus of our ministry. No one has sinned too much. No one is less worthy than another. Everyone must be valued and targeted for discipleship ministries. If an individual is left out, the church is not doing its job correctly.

True Discipleship Is Primary

Understanding that every individual is valued and important is only the first half of a bigger issue. It is equally critical to focus on what the church is doing with those individuals. We noted that in areas of disciple making the church is struggling. How important is this issue?

Biblical evidence indicates that disciple making is of extreme interest to God. The call to make disciples is not an arbitrary task that is added to some other function. Rather, it is the foundational command of Christ in His Great Commission (Matthew 28:19).

Consider for a moment those individuals who are a part of your class or congregation. Every teacher and leader must answer the following questions as they relate to the individuals they are helping to disciple:

1. Do the lifestyles of these people reflect the principles and character of Christ?
2. What percentage of these people are easily shaken in their faith or vulnerable to deceitful schemes?

3. Do they mutually edify and build up one another?
4. In what ways are they ministering?

These inquiries reflect the true nature of the church's mission. These questions, and others like them, must be answered.

A disciple is a learner or follower who reflects the pattern of the one being followed and is able to reproduce that pattern in others. Is that what we are producing?

Many people come and go through the doors of a local church, but how many are becoming disciples? Disciple making is Christ's central command and the ultimate task of the local church, but is it happening?

The local church and its leadership must recognize the biblical priority placed on the individual. The local church can measure its success by the spiritual growth of the individual. Any other measure lacks the commission Christ gave to the disciples and His church. The local church and the Church universal must clearly understand that its highest goal is to build people.

But how does the local church take on or re-energize this priority? The remainder of this book is dedicated to such a pursuit. In the chapters ahead, a full strategy for building people will unfold. Every local church leader, teacher, or worker can be a successful "people builder" for the kingdom of God.

Steps Toward Valuing the Individual

The first step toward building people must be a renewed focus on the individual. In previous pages we discussed why such a focus is necessary. Let us now consider three steps needed to accomplish this priority.

Know the Individual

One of the most remarkable passages of Scripture tells us, "'Even the very hairs of your head are all numbered'" (Matthew 10:30). What an incredible picture of God's genuine, detailed interest in the individual. With such evidence, who could doubt that God knows our individual needs and is concerned with those things that concern us? Indeed, in light of such a verse, it is not difficult to believe in God's providential care and specific plan for every individual.

This same principle must be evident in the care the local church extends to each person. A pastor, Sunday school teacher, or other discipler cannot know the individual with the depth of knowledge the Creator does. Nonetheless, only through significant knowledge of the individual can effective strategies for discipleship be developed.

Let's return to Jackie, our single mother with two teenage boys. What individual needs might she have? Can a local church minister to her effectively without getting to know her?

Perhaps in conversation, Jackie would reveal a financial crisis, a difficulty she is having with one of her sons, a struggle with her custody or support arrangements, a prolonged loneliness or lack of friendships, or a belief that no one really cares. Even if Jackie is well adjusted to her circumstances and every relationship is running smoothly, she is still an individual with her own special needs.

Jackie is also at a unique point in her spiritual need. Perhaps she is unsaved or a new Christian. Maybe she has confusion in some doctrinal areas or has a desire to use her talented singing voice in music ministry. Who knows? Unless an effort is made to know Jackie, she will only be a single face among the masses, and the very purposes of the church will go unfulfilled in her life.

Knowledge of the individual is a "turf" issue. The worship service is the pastor's turf. The Sunday school class is the teacher's turf. Most of the people who come into the local church dress and act according to the rules of the local church turf. Notice a Sunday morning worship service. Most of the people are dressed similarly, according to the standard established by the group. Most conduct themselves within a tight parameter of expectations. They sing when everyone sings, stand when everyone stands, laugh when everyone laughs, and pray when everyone prays. Even those who do not participate in the activity of the group still behave in similar ways as the crowd. Corporate worship is not typically a time for individual expression.

Can church leaders truly come to know people in such a setting? Not likely. It becomes imperative that people be met on their turf, where they determine their own dress, behavior, and activity. On their own turf is where people will be themselves. On their own turf is where people can be known.

Such a reality of turf calls the youth leader to a high school basketball game or some other place where his teens gather. A children's teacher or worker may choose to visit her students in their homes or at a playground. A pastor or adult leader may join one of his people in a corporate cafeteria in order to know him better. Ultimately the goal is to meet people on their own turf so their individual characteristics and needs may become known.

Target Relationship Building

While Jesus dealt frequently with crowds, the greater effect of His mission was on the lives of those with whom He built relationships. He fed thousands with a boy's lunch, but it was His closest followers who changed the world. For the church to accomplish life-change in its members, relationships must become a priority.

Human beings were made for relationship. This very need prompted the Creator to give Adam and Eve to one another. People's need for relationship has not changed. It is a primary motive in decision making and life choices. Nothing is so central to people as their need of others.

In modern society, traditional relationships have broken down. Marital relationships frequently shatter. Parent-child relationships continue to deteriorate. Some modern cultural ideas claim personal independence, doubting the necessity of relationships. But the evidence weighs heavily on the other side. The more we spurn relationships, the more we find we need them.

Today's children and teens bear the brunt of this weakening of relationships. Often money and possessions are presented as a substitute, but the need for relationship only intensifies. Listen to the words of one teen: "We do not need a BMW. We do not need a summer cottage. We do not need tailor-made clothes. What we do need and want is a cohesive family unit."[5]

The people who attend a local church are increasingly in need of relationship. For many the traditional home is shattered. Their family, designed by God to provide belonging, is no longer available. The greatest opportunity for the church to affect their lives is through relationship.

In a smaller congregation, such a priority can be accomplished through friendliness and occasional fellowship activities. For the larger church, however, a more concerted effort becomes necessary. Small-group activities, support groups for those facing similar struggles, family activities, and significant personal care are some of the possibilities. Regardless of size, a church that provides no means by which relationships can be built is not exhibiting a focus on the individual.

Relationship is critical to the ministry of disciple making. The apostle Paul encouraged those he was discipling, "Follow my example, as I follow the example of Christ" (1 Corinthians 11:1). This can be accomplished only through relationship.

Teach To Meet Needs

The final step in turning toward the individual involves effort in the classroom or sanctuary setting. Like those who lived in Jesus' day, today's individuals want to have their needs addressed. They want to know the Bible's guidance in a job circumstance. They want to understand the Christian approach to a decision they face. They want specific encouragement in their difficulties and specific prayer for their needs.

When the teacher or leader has come to know the student

and has built a relationship with the student, the teacher or leader can target ministry accurately for the benefit of the student. In pulpit ministry, a pastor who knows his or her people and has built relationships with many of them also knows their spiritual needs and the areas of personal growth that are on the horizon. Such knowledge serves as a wonderful guide for planning both message and ministries.

Teaching to meet needs involves all aspects of discipleship. As a teacher prepares a lesson, those who will be taught must be considered. Various aspects of the lesson should receive greater priority according to the needs of the students. Those same needs should also dictate the direction of the response time or closing prayer.

Such a targeting of needs also helps overcome limited resources. For example, Debbie is a sixth-grade Sunday school teacher. She has spent many months building relationships with the 11 boys and girls in her class. She has learned that these students have a good understanding of the Bible and excel in Scripture memory. The earlier years of Sunday school training coupled with above average parental involvement have paid dividends.

Debbie also sees that many of her students struggle socially. While most can quote 1 Corinthians 13, few are adept at making friends. How should Debbie spend the limited resources set aside for this class? A social activity would probably be a good choice. Maybe a pizza party at her own home or a trip to a nearby amusement park. Why? Because Debbie knows what her class needs.

If the scenario were reversed and the class had strong social skills but limited scriptural knowledge and understanding, would Debbie's decision be different? Certainly. Debbie would then spend those limited resources according to her students' greater need.

Ultimately, teaching to meet and target needs means letting the knowledge of the individual sway the direction of all efforts. Such a direction is not to teach people what they want to hear—a frightful sign of the end time (2 Timothy 4:3).

Direction of effort provides the ministry and teaching they need to hear.

Can it be done? Can the individual become the true focus of local church ministry? Perhaps the opposite question should be asked. Can the church afford to neglect the individual? Perhaps a final example will cement the point.

Suppose that final example is you. Ask yourself these questions:

"Who was the first person to make me feel valued and important in my local church? What effect did his or her effort of personal investment have on my life? What other people have extended friendship to me within the body of Christ? Did their friendship help make my own involvement a higher priority?" Each individual is valued; . . . the focus of each individual in our ministry.

Now ask, "Who around me is unimportant to God? How can I affect the individuals around me? Who are the people I can help build?"

And then remember that each individual is valued; each individual is the focus of your ministry.

---

[1]Edythe Draper, *Draper's Book of Quotations* (Wheaton, Ill.: Tyndale House Publishers, 1992), 335.

[2]Adapted from George Barna, *Today's Pastors* (Ventura, Calif.: Regal Books, 1993), 135–36.

[3]From a presentation by Steve Mills, one of the authors of this book.

[4]Barna, *Today's Pastors*, 101.

[5]William Mahedy and Janet Bernardi, *A Generation Alone* (Downers Grove, Ill.: Intervarsity Press, 1994), 19.

2
Values and Principles

Every man is worth just so much as the things are worth about which he busies himself.
—Marcus Aurelius Antoninus

Values. We all have them. They serve as an internal compass directing every attitude, decision, and priority of our lives. Values are the ultimate decision makers that huddle at the core of our hearts. They are the filter through which we see, act, and react. Determine a person's values and you have determined the person.

In spite of the fundamental nature of values in our lives, few people ever actually identify or intentionally shape their values. Few ever ask, "What are my values?" This important question leads to remarkable self-revelation.

Let's look at a few examples. A dad who cancels a late-night business meeting to attend a child's school play reveals his own values. His behavior states to those who observe his decision, "My child is a significant priority which I place above the demands of my work."

Suppose a mother spends an entire Saturday in the sweltering heat of a Little League ballpark watching her child compete in a baseball tournament. Her behavior reveals her values. Perhaps her values could be stated as, "My physical comfort is less important to me than being a part of my child's activities." Or suppose a mother spends an entire night caring for her sleepless infant. Again, her values are revealed.

The opposite behavior is equally revealing. If that same father continually places responsibilities and opportunities at work ahead of time with his family, his actions state a different set of values. If the mother in the example fails to attend the baseball tournament in favor of her own activities, she conveys an unfortunate set of values to her child.

In spite of what we say is important, our behavior reveals our values. If we say that our children are the most important priority in our lives, but our behavior is directed toward other areas, we reveal that our true values do not match our claims.

Values cover a much wider spectrum than simply our attitudes toward family relationships. How we function on the job, in marital relationships, among our friends, or how we participate in church and in spiritual growth are dictated by our values. Every role we fill in this life is affected significantly by our values.

Let's focus here on collective values. What are the values of a church? What values guide the discipleship efforts of a local church or Sunday school team? What values motivate teachers or workers as they invest themselves in their students? Essentially, what guides our thinking and activity in the making of disciples?

We established a key value statement in chapter 1: Every individual is valued and is the focus of our ministry. As we said, this is the cornerstone of building people. This value statement should be seen in our ministry effort; our behavior should reflect the true evidence of this value.

In this chapter, we want to look at four additional value statements that are essential to making disciples. These four statements help us summarize the priority of four key areas in the effort to build people. While our central focus is on the individual, these four statements define what a disciple-making church hopes to accomplish in the life of each individual. The following pages provide simply an overview; a full presentation of any of these statements would be a book in itself.

Understanding the Gospel

The first of these value statements focuses specific attention on the central purpose of Jesus Christ and His church—the purpose of evangelism.

> Value Statement #1
>
> Every person has the right to a presentation of the gospel at his or her level of understanding.

This essential belief is the motivation of virtually all efforts of ministry. Evangelism is the initial step of discipleship and must always be a priority in the local church. To lose track of such a priority turns a church inward, focusing on itself and ultimately slipping into decline.

The emphasis is on the individual's level of understanding. The statement does not accept a blanket presentation of the gospel. Only a tailor-made effort is acceptable. Foreign missions efforts or cross-cultural ministries make this point clear. It is also because of this belief that the gospel is presented in a way that children can understand its concepts. Because the individual is the priority, effort must be made to help the learning disabled to grasp the gospel's concepts. Teens may also require a presentation of the gospel that addresses their specific needs and hopes. If we believe the statement that "every person has the right to a presentation of the gospel at his or her level of understanding," such a belief will propel us to the work necessary to make it happen.

The Bible as the Answer

To establish the value statement, "Every person has a right to a presentation of the gospel at his or her level of understanding," certain supporting principles must be understood and accepted. The relationship of these principles to our value statement can best be understood by defining *principles* as "statements we know are true" and *values* as "those responses that we make based on the principles."

One such principle is the following:

Principle #1: The timeless message of the Bible is the answer to human need.

A quick look at the neighborhood, at the community, at the headlines, or at a television newscast will reveal that people have a plethora of needs. Rising rates of violence, sexual promiscuity, abuse, and disease, coupled with the high-speed decline of family relationships, personal integrity, and morality keep the desperate needs of people quite visible. Today technologies easily outrace our ability to answer the ethical questions they raise. The very fabric of society seems to unravel further every day.

In this day of modern problems, is there a modern solution? While medical science has provided us with new and difficult questions to answer, hasn't it also brought answers to ancient problems? What about the information highway? Hasn't this fast-paced technology brought some solutions to the challenges we face?

The answer may seem to be "yes" to some issues and areas of need, but an honest evaluation must conclude that modern problems are growing faster than modern solutions. Gadgets designed to make life easier have brought little relief. Stress continues to rise in spite of increased monitoring and treatment. Human beings have not found the solution to their needs in any modern effort.

As Christians, we know that the Bible continues to provide the solutions for every generation. What modern people need is a not-so-modern answer.

The principle under consideration is an essential truth for every teacher or worker. The message of the Bible is timeless; it is relevant for every generation. If a teacher is discipling inner-city children, that teacher must believe that the Bible is the valid resource for the challenges those children face. If a person is discipling a single mother, the source for answers is the same. Though there may be literally thousands of circumstances and situations, the Christian leader knows that there is only one source of true hope—the Bible.

Today's church faces the temptation to accept the latest surge of new ideas and concepts as its solution for the problems in people's lives. Trendy attitudes and ideas may be more popular than the Bible at first, but their shallow nature will soon reveal their inadequacy. Nearly 3,000 years ago the Psalmist shared his conclusion: "The precepts of the Lord are right, giving joy to the heart. The commands of the Lord are radiant, giving light to the eyes" (Psalm 19:8).

Though our problems today may look quite different from those of the ancient shepherd, our final conclusion is the same: The timeless message of the Bible is the answer to human need.

Christ's Priority

A large part of prayer for most Christians consists of our desire to have God respond to the list of requests that we want or need answered. Have you ever wondered if God had a list He wanted to show us? If so, what kind of requests would God make of us?

The answer is in the Bible. At the very top of God's list is the salvation of each individual. Listen to these words: "The Son of Man came to seek and to save what was lost" (Luke 19:10). "He is patient with you, not wanting anyone to perish, but everyone to come to repentance" (2 Peter 3:9).

The second principle that undergirds our belief that "every person has a right to a presentation of the gospel at his or her level of understanding," focuses on this priority of our Lord and Master. It is presented in the following statement:

Principle #2: The priority of Christ and His church is the salvation of each individual.

No Bible-believing Christian could argue with this principle. Why must every individual be given an opportunity to understand and respond to the gospel? Because this is the primary objective of our Creator's redemptive plan.

It is beyond our mere human thinking to even begin to understand the intensity of Christ's priority here. For this He came, and for this He died. The excruciating agony of the cross did not deter Him. He knowingly faced that hideous day because His objective had been laid before Him. The salvation of each individual drove the entire redemptive plan. Nothing else took priority.

While Christ's total dedication to the salvation of each individual is clear, His intent was also that His church share that conviction. In Matthew 28:19,20, Jesus passes the baton of this eternal mission to His followers: "'Go and make disciples of all nations, baptizing them in the name of the Father and of the Son and of the Holy Spirit, and teaching them to obey everything I have commanded you. And surely I am with you always, to the very end of the age.'"

Notice that Christ not only commissioned His followers but also promised to go with them. Why? There is no question that they would need Him and the power of the Holy Spirit. But there is an additional reason why He promised His presence: making disciples is His mission. He was not abandoning the task to them, but rather bringing them into His mission, a mission He continues to serve even now.

That this is Christ's mission is beyond question. Perhaps a more difficult question is whether or not this remains the Church's mission. Each local church must answer this question. To build people, it is absolutely essential that the local church commit to this mission of making disciples. This is the true starting point, the point of life-change. Without this mission, the church becomes just another social gathering or neighborhood club.

Character and Caring

Can you remember your favorite high school textbook? Such a question is more likely to receive a laugh than an answer.

Few of us can remember any high school textbook, much less recall a favorite.

Suppose we change the question. Can you remember your favorite high school teacher? Now the images flood to mind. Answers immediately present themselves as we think back to an individual who made learning fun, challenged us personally, or just seemed to think we mattered. We remember the teacher as strong in character and seemingly always focused on helping us.

Why did the teacher make a difference? While our value statement, "Every person has a right to a presentation of the gospel at his or her level of understanding," says something about the importance of the gospel and about the priority of the individual, it also says something about us. Our third and final supporting principle refers to the teacher:

Principle #3: We influence first by our character and caring and then by what we communicate.

That high school teacher affected our lives because of his or her character and caring. The teacher's individual investment in our lives helped us learn and made us want to learn. The character, the worthiness of respect, the caring, and the individual interest in us opened the door for us to accept what the teacher had to teach us.

The same is true in building people. Sunday school teachers may prepare remarkable lessons, but that isn't enough. A credibility gap must be bridged. Today's teachers must prove they are worthy of attention. Such worthiness is established not by the strength of what they communicate, but by the evidence of their own lives and by their genuine concern for their students.

From which individual will a child learn more, a skilled orator or a loving nurturer? The answer is obvious. That answer doesn't change as we grow older. We respond to those we respect, trust, and feel care about us.

In a day when trust and credibility have become harder to locate, the need for these traits has intensified. Individuals have broken trust in all walks of life. Trust in government officials, business people, educators, and even church leaders steadily declines. Yet, the need to build such trust remains. When an individual finds a leader or teacher whose character can be trusted, an opportunity for teaching is born. In our efforts for the kingdom of God, trustworthy character is essential.

One cannot underestimate the value of caring either. A familiar quote emphasizes the point: "People don't care what you know until they know that you care."

As teachers of the greatest message ever taught, we must prove to people the genuineness of our care before we can expect them to listen. It may take a teacher of adults an entire year of faithfulness and friendship before students begin to respond. The time period is usually shorter for teens and children since they tend to trust more quickly. For every trust relationship that has been broken in the past, the period of proving is extended.

Before an individual will hear and respond to a presentation of the gospel and any future effort of discipling, character and caring must be proven. The question, "Why should I listen to you?" must be answered. In this generation where relationships crumble frequently, the validity of this principle is even more evident.

The Bible is the answer, salvation of every individual is the priority, and people of character and caring are necessary to communicate the eternal mission of Christ to their world.

A Moral Compass

Have you ever been lost? The challenge of steering the car with one leg while using both hands to wrestle a road map is one we've all faced. Street signs fly by, never matching the name of the road we are looking for. Only after significant frustration will we admit failure and stop to ask directions of someone who is familiar with the road.

Life is often like that too. Today's combination of violence, terror, stress, family deterioration, and emotional wreckage makes even the strongest among us long for some direction. Where can we turn? Our second of four value statements provides the answer.

> **Value Statement #2**
>
> Every person needs a biblical, moral compass to guide and protect him or her throughout life.

We established that the Bible is the answer for human need, but we must also remember that the Bible provides a pattern for living. As leaders in the local church, we recognize that this is the pattern we must teach and model for those whom we lead. The heart of discipleship is helping a follower of Christ understand and obey the direction of that compass.

Three supporting principles will affirm our value statement. Remember, the principles are the statements we know are true and values are those responses we make based on the principles.

A Lifelong Process

The first of these principles is as follows:

Principle #1: Personal growth is a lifelong process.

While the Bible does provide us with the compass needed for life with Christ, the pathway encompasses an entire life. The arrival point does not occur in this lifetime, but rather in the life to come. The apostle John describes it this way: "Dear friends, now we are children of God, and what we will be has not yet been made known. But we know that when he appears, we shall be like him, for we shall see him as he is" (1 John 3:2).

For the church then, building people is for everyone. The investment in the individual is needed for all. People of all ages, backgrounds, abilities, and experiences require that biblical compass. Such a belief calls us to disciple the youngest child and the oldest adult. While individuals mature in their walk with Christ and become less dependent on the leadership of others, still the path winds ahead.

The Sunday school is one structure that understands this principle. People are discipled from the cradle to the grave. There is no inherent attitude or belief that some have arrived or achieved the highest plateau. We build people for life.

Belief in building for life brings perspective. The apostle Paul calls his walk with Christ a "race." It is not a sprint or dash, but a marathon that requires faithful effort all the way. Here are Paul's familiar words as his life neared its end: "I have fought the good fight, I have finished the race, I have kept the faith" (2 Timothy 4:7).

This is the testimony of one who ran strong all the way to the end. Paul knew that his own personal growth had been a lifelong journey.

The Role of Parents

Another principle that the Bible provides concerns the intended avenue of discipleship. If the Bible is a moral compass, whose task is it to show the way? Certainly, a strong case can be made for the church. Jesus entrusted His followers with the truth of His message and the command to reproduce themselves in others. Without question, the local church is a critical dispenser of direction and guidance for the individual.

The Bible does, however, emphasize the importance of another institution in the communication of God's purposes and plans—the family. Hear the instruction given through Moses:

> These commandments that I give you today are to be upon your hearts. Impress them on your children. Talk about them when you sit at home and when you walk along the road, when you lie down and when you get up. Tie them as symbols on your hands and bind them on your foreheads. Write them on the door frames of your houses and on your gates (Deuteronomy 6:6-9).

Quite thorough, isn't it? The command leaves the impression that children are to see the direction and the commands of God everywhere they look!

The point is clear. Parents are at the center of God's planned methodology for perpetuating His people. Our principle statement says it this way:

Principle #2: Parents are their children's first and primary teachers.

Any brief observation of human behavior reveals the enormous influence that parents have on their children, either for good or for bad. Parents are the single greatest influence in a child's life. No individual, whether by cunning or by caring, can replace the role of a parent in a child's life.

While our purpose here is not a detailed discussion of this relationship, it is imperative that we recognize the family as the primary thread in the fabric of our society. The modern deterioration of the family and the corresponding moral decline of our society give evidence of the importance of this biblical institution.

Since the primary role of the parent is a biblical fact, what should be the response of the local church? If parents play such a key role both in the commands of God and in the influence of their children, then building parents must become a key strategy for discipleship. A local church that builds a strong ministry to children can take advantage of its greatest opportunity to have a long-term influence on their lives by building an equally strong training program for parents.

Small Groups

The final principle to guide us in presenting this moral compass relates to the structure of our efforts. While we determined that the process is lifelong and the family is the key unit for discipleship, what principle should govern the church's own efforts of discipleship? Consider this:

Principle #3: Acceptance, caring, and learning occur best in small groups.

Jesus showed us this principle in Luke 6:13 when, from among the many who followed Him, He selected a group of 12. These men were given more intensive teaching and personal investment. Even among the 12, a smaller group of 3 were chosen—Peter, James, and John. They were with Jesus during the events on the Mount of Transfiguration and in the Garden of Gethsemane.

Why did Jesus use the small group? The answer must come from our own experience of the effectiveness of small groups. The Sunday school, the most familiar of the church's small-group efforts, has proven its ability to build people. The small-group interaction, the targeting of personal needs, and the possibility of individual investment accomplish much life-change.

The small group provides greater opportunities for personal belonging than can be provided by the larger setting. People who feel needed and included are far superior in their faithfulness, accountability, and individual growth than those who have no such feelings.

Many churches have found that the small-group structure facilitates all areas of ministry. Care structures, fellowship programs, and teaching ministries all benefit from the small group. Where the local church has abandoned or de-emphasized the small group in favor of the larger, more enthusiastic crowd, the opportunity for true life-change and discipleship is greatly diminished and the longevity of the church's ministry is significantly threatened.

Consider the words of noted church growth observer, John Vaughn: "Churches that generate their worship attendance growth through the continued creation of new multiple worship services, without also creating additional small groups (i.e., Sunday school classes and/or home cell groups), are in danger of building the empty cathedrals of the next generation."[1]

The Priesthood of the Believer

The third of four value statements under consideration is as follows.

Value Statement #3

Every believer has unique gifts to be developed and used to strengthen the church.

Do you remember Scott, our young college graduate from chapter 1? He and Jackie, along with the Kellys, helped us see the importance of the individual to Christ and to the local church. Why are they important? They and every other individual are priorities because of their right to an understandable presentation of the gospel and because of their need for a moral compass to guide and protect them.

The Scriptures take us a step farther. Each of these individuals also has a purpose and a place in the eternal plan of God. Scott has been equipped by his Creator with certain gifts that are to be used in service to God. So has Jackie. Even the youngest of the Kellys has gifts and abilities to be used for the glory of God.

Let's look at three key principles that help undergird this important value statement. Remember that the principles are the statements we know are true and the values are those responses that we make based on the principles.

Obedience and Worship

Consider the first principle:

Principle #1: Obedience is the essence of discipleship and the highest form of worship.

Jesus said, "'If anyone loves me, he will obey my teaching. . . . He who does not love me will not obey my teaching'" (John 14:23,24).

With this simple yet profound statement, Jesus establishes the firm link between obedience and worship.

One of the most remarkable challenges of the Christian life is communicating our love to God. Having experienced the marvel of His love for us, we are left with the immense task of loving Him in return. Indeed, loving God is singled out by the

Bible as the greatest of all the commandments (Matthew 22:37,38).

How are we to love God? Verbal communication of our love through praise is described as a fragrant aroma to His heavenly throne. Yet Jesus repeatedly establishes that the most effective way to communicate our love to God is through our obedience to those things He has commanded.

Much like the father who watches his own child obey his direction, our Heavenly Father relishes that same obedience from each of His children. "If you love me, obey me," comes the instruction.

As disciplers, this instruction has a dual impact. First, it is relevant to our own lives. We dare not abandon the call to obedience ourselves. Second, we must recognize this command in the life of the one we disciple. As teachers, leaders, or workers, we must make known the opportunity and help guide the student into that obedience.

The Church's Responsibility

The second principle drives the point closer to home. Consider it carefully:

Principle #2: Responsibility for equipping the believer is vested in the church.

A familiar passage from the apostle Paul establishes this principle: He . . . gave some to be apostles, some to be prophets, some to be evangelists, and some to be pastors and teachers, to prepare God's people for works of service, so that the body of Christ may be built up until we all reach unity in the faith and in the knowledge of the Son of God and become mature, attaining to the whole measure of the fullness of Christ (Ephesians 4:11–13).

It is the responsibility of the local church to help every Scott and Jackie discover and develop his or her gifts of ministry for the benefit of the whole body. This must be a major part of the effort to build people.

The modern church suffers tragically from a spectator mentality. Too many people are watching; too few people are doing. Researchers, such as George Barna, have interviewed pastors and other church leaders about their greatest frustrations. Leading the list is the lack of commitment among the lay members.[2] The pastor or church leader who tries to compensate for this lack ends up serving approximately 80 percent of the members who are spectators in the church. Attempting to assist the pastor are the 20 percent of the members who do 80 percent of the ministry. The result is a tragically ineffective church that fails to reflect the direction of the apostle to help all believers develop their gifts.

In the effective church, however, the pastor and other leaders equip the 20 percent to lead the 80 percent who do the ministry of the church. The effective church serves God by serving people. Its leaders know they are responsible for developing disciples. The difference between the effective church and the ineffective church is Scott, the spectator. If Scott only watches and feeds off the efforts of others, then the church is ineffective. If Scott becomes a part of those serving by investing himself in the work and finding a place where he can get involved, then the church has moved toward effectiveness in Scott's life as well as in the lives of all whom Scott will help serve.

The 80/20 principle, also called the Pareto Principle, shows the benefits of building people.

The Biblical Leader

The third and final principle for this value statement concerns the content of equipping. While equipping for ministry is necessary and is the responsibility of the local church, what characteristics must be built?

Consider the following principle:

Principle #3: Biblical leadership requires servanthood and godly character, as well as ministry skills.

As stated earlier, character and caring must precede content in effective ministry. This is true for the discipler and is an essential part of the training for the disciple. Jesus emphasized the point clearly: "'You know that those who are regarded as rulers of the Gentiles lord it over them, and their high officials exercise authority over them. Not so with you. Instead, whoever wants to become great among you must be your servant, and whoever wants to be first must be slave of all. For even the Son of Man did not come to be served, but to serve, and to give his life as a ransom for many'" (Mark 10:42–45).

Suppose Jackie has a marvelous gift of musical ability and Scott has potential as a teacher. What kind of servants will they be? They must be guided in the development of their gifts, but they also must be guided in their servanthood. Of what benefit is it to the kingdom of God if Jackie's marvelous voice attracts crowds only to worship Jackie? Of what value is Scott's teaching ability if he fails to care for his students the way Christ would? Would either of them reflect the One of whom they sing and teach?

In serving Christ the attitude is more crucial than the action; the person is more crucial than the performance. Scott should be molded into the best possible teacher for the glory of his Savior, but we must be certain that all training effort be done to mold a servant whose primary goal is godly character.

A Global Mission

The value statements we have considered thus far reflect what we believe about each individual. This final statement is no exception.

> Value Statement #4
>
> Every believer has a purpose in advancing the global mission of the church of Jesus Christ.

Becky was shy, soft-spoken, and slightly overweight at 19. Seldom would she be pried from the middle of the pack at any social function. She just blended in among the crowd, never calling attention to herself or to her abilities. Few people even noticed her. But every Sunday morning, Becky held the attention of seven fifth-grade girls with her inspired teaching of the Bible.

Dave wasn't very outgoing either, but the third-grade boys had never had a teacher like him. He combined his timid voice with the gifted strokes of an artist's paintbrush into a life-changing encounter with God's Word in every Sunday's lesson.

Bill was a confirmed bachelor. His life revolved around no one but himself—except for the boys he taught every Wednesday night. Bill's years of camping and survival training opened just the right opportunities to share his love for Christ with these boys. Bill never had kids of his own, but, after 11 years of Wednesday nights, he had helped shape many young lives.

Who are these people? They're the Scotts and the Jackies who have found their place in the global mission of Jesus Christ. They're in the disciple-making business themselves now. Most of them are working far beyond their natural abilities or experiences, and the results are equally supernatural. Let's look at three principles that brought them there.

The Believer's Commission

Read again Christ's parting words, recorded by Matthew: "'Go and make disciples of all nations, baptizing them in the name of the Father and of the Son and of the Holy Spirit, and teaching them to obey everything I have commanded you. And surely I am with you always, to the very end of the age'" (Matthew 28:19,20).

This mission of Christ was imparted to the Church. Let's take one step farther. The first principle concerning Christ's mission brings the challenge down to the individual:

Principle #1: Every believer is commissioned by God to make disciples.

The discipleship process comes full circle. The Scotts and Jackies are to be discipled, then they are to become disciple makers themselves. What a marvelous moment in the life of every follower of Christ when the mission becomes their own and a lifelong course is set for building people. Disciples making disciples is the process that has perpetuated the church of Jesus Christ throughout its 2,000 years.

Individuals like Becky, Dave, and Bill prove that our place in the mission is not limited by age or natural ability. As with David, Gideon, and others in the Bible, the Creator knows the gifts He has invested.

The Power of the Spirit

The second principle concerns the equipping for the mission. Consider the following statement:

Principle #2: Spirit baptism is a priority for Great Commission service.

As Pentecostals, we have long recognized the supernatural equipping provided by the Holy Spirit. The entire Book of Acts records the marvelous works of the Holy Spirit in the early days of the Church. The supernatural was commonplace where the Holy Spirit was in evidence. Even today that same supernatural power is evident. As Acts 1:8 points out, there is power to be witnesses when we experience the baptism in the Spirit.

While few Pentecostals would question the availability of a Spirit baptism today, many miss the priority placed on this equipping by Jesus himself: "'Do not leave Jerusalem, but wait for the gift my Father promised, which you have heard me speak about. For John baptized with water, but in a few days you will be baptized with the Holy Spirit'" (Acts 1:4,5).

The Holy Spirit is the primary equipment for Christ's mission. Notice His command to wait. He knew that prior to their experience of the Holy Spirit they were ill-equipped to fulfill His mission. Once this Spirit baptism had been received, they were to embark on His mission.

The Holy Spirit's equipping is what brings the remarkable from the Beckys and the Daves. It is what propels people like Bill, with their experience and expertise, into God-charted service. The definition of the mission is disciples making disciples, and the equipment of the mission is the power of the Holy Spirit.

The Motivation for Service

The final principle provides the motivation for the mission. While we established worship as a key motivation in obedience, Jesus gives us a further motive as evidenced in this principle:

Principle #3: Awareness of need is a primary motivation for Great Commission service.

Jesus' words, recorded in John's Gospel, provide the foundation for this final principle: "'Do you not say, "Four months more and then the harvest"? I tell you, open your eyes and look at the fields! They are ripe for harvest. Even now the reaper draws his wages, even now he harvests the crop for eternal life, so that the sower and the reaper may be glad together'" (John 4:35,36).

It is not difficult to find application of this passage in today's world. Even the briefest glance reveals a world full of enormous need and great opportunity to find a place for fulfilling the mission of Christ. There is ample work to be done and a place for every individual to be involved.

Tommy Barnett, pastor of First Assembly of God, Phoenix, Arizona, has often shared the basic philosophy of his years of growing some of the nation's largest congregations. His philosophy is simple: "Find a need and meet it!"

Hundreds of disciples have done exactly that. By the power of the Holy Spirit and with the priority of making disciples, they have spotted opportunity for service and found their place in the mission. This is the hope of the church for every individual. Each student in a Sunday school classroom is part of the mission. For every child, for every teen, and for every adult there is a place of service.

Summary

This is the "why" of building people. It is not enough to assemble en masse for just another cause. Today's church must become the life-change station it is eternally intended to be. Why? Because . . .

Every person is valued and is the focus of our ministry.

Every person has the right to a presentation of the gospel at his or her level of understanding.

Every person needs a biblical, moral compass to guide and protect him or her throughout life.

Every believer has unique gifts to be developed and used to strengthen the church.

Every believer has a purpose in advancing the global mission of the church of Jesus Christ.

These two introductory chapters provide an overview of the values that drive a disciple-making church. Now we will consider the precise vision and strategy to accomplish this task of building people.

---

[1]John Vaughn, *Megachurches and America's Cities* (Grand Rapids: Baker Book House, 1993), 58.

[2]George Barna, *Today's Pastors* (Ventura, Calif.: Regal Books, 1993), 66.

3
The Model for Discipleship

A task without a vision is drudgery; a vision without a task is a dream; a task with a vision is victory.
—*Anonymous*[1]

The bat cracks and the excited crowd rises to cheer. A player trots around the three bases and turns toward home plate. Jubilant teammates wait to congratulate the batter who has hit the game winner, and thousands share in the accomplishment.

Individual effort, developed by a coach and supported by a team, makes baseball the sport of choice for millions. The baseball diamond is an appropriate model for understanding the disciple-making process. If we think of Becky, Dave, Bill, and others as the base runners, we readily realize that a strategy is essential for moving them from first to second to third base and then home.

As we focus on the person as the object of ministry, the need for a community is apparent. In a disciple-building community, the person finds Christ, builds life-changing relationships with other believers, matures in the spiritual disciplines, discovers the gifts Christ has entrusted to believers, and finds a place to serve in the eternal plan of God.

Disciple—Noun and Verb

Before we study the disciple-making process, we ought to come to a consensus on what a disciple is and what it means to disciple. In an address to Christian educators, Billie Davis observed that *disciple* is a unique word that can be both a noun and a verb. As a noun, she defined the word to mean "one who not only learns from a master but also helps to propagate the teachings."

> Students can learn for their own benefit but need not agree with the teachings nor accept their teacher's philosophies and values. The word pupil originally meant a younger person under the control of a teaching master. Even the words follower and learner have meanings that are not exactly interchangeable with disciple. A disciple has a personal commitment to the master, a sense of being called to help perpetuate his teachings.
>
> Disciple as a verb means perpetuation, disciples making disciples. No other word is like it. Other nouns have been made into verbs; for example, parenting, mothering, and ministering. But a parent parents a child. Making mothers is not essential to the idea of mothering. To minister may be an end in itself.
>
> Disciple is different. The unique concept of disciple is that it makes being and doing one. This is the inherent nature of Christianity. You disciple to make disciples, and you are not a disciple if you do not disciple.[2]

Disciple as a noun and as a verb is integral to our study. We will look at the decisions a person makes to become a disciple and at the strategies a church employs to disciple those persons entrusted to its care. Our diamond model serves as a means for tracing the development of the disciple and for evaluating the church's effectiveness as a disciple-making community.

Disciple—The Noun

How do people become disciples? The first step is to be *committed to membership.* At Base 1 in our model, people decide to be joined in relationship with Christ through salvation and joined to a local church through friendship. The model helps us to recognize when people have reached this point. We know they are committed to membership when people

1. Know what sin is and why humankind needs a Savior. This knowledge is personalized so that people realize they are sinners and come to God seeking forgiveness. They further seek to symbolize their conversion through water baptism.

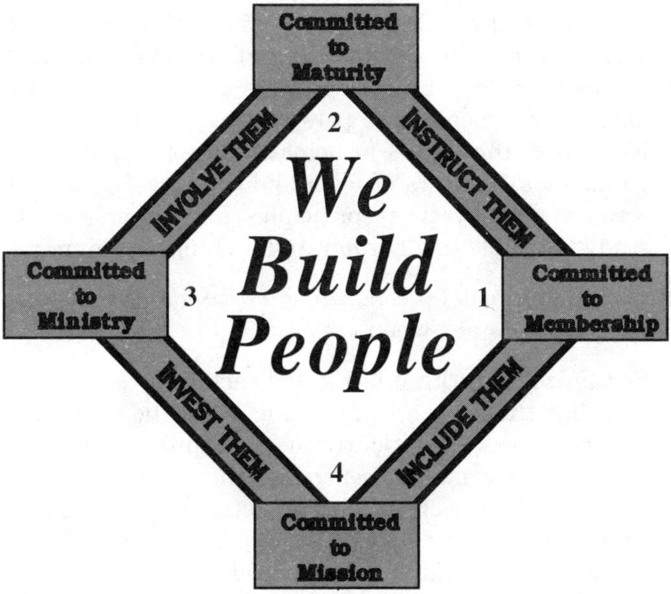

2. Know that the church is Christ's body and is the family of God that is to fulfill a threefold mission in the world: worship, edification, and evangelism. They recognize the value of Christian fellowship and join the fellowship of believers in a consistent pattern of attendance.
3. Know that the Bible is the divinely inspired, infallible revelation of God to humankind. They value and respect the Scriptures and use them to investigate claims concerning the Christian faith.

At Base 2, people become *committed to maturity.* We know they have moved to this commitment when they

1. Know that the baptism in the Holy Spirit is for all believers and that it brings supernatural power for life as a witness. In response to this knowledge, they seek the baptism in the Holy Spirit, and, subsequent to this infilling, they enter into a Spirit-filled life.
2. Know that Christlikeness is the aim of the Christian life. They desire to live a Christlike life that is evidenced by (a) love for God, (b) love for others, and (c) a consistent pattern of corporate and personal prayer and worship.
3. Know that the Bible's principles and commands provide guidance in matters of faith and conduct. Because they want to live by these principles and commands, they study the Bible in a regular and systematic manner.

Base 3 in our model is *commitment to ministry.* People have moved on to this stage when they

1. Recognize that Christ has gifted each believer for service and that the church cannot function without everyone's participation. Consequently, they recognize their accountability as servants and contribute their time, talents, and material possessions to the ministry efforts of the local church.
2. Know that greatness is measured by servanthood and therefore exhibit a spirit of humility and teachability in the service of others.
3. Know that Christian service is done more effectively through united rather than individual efforts.

Base 4, the ultimate goal of the discipling process, is a *commitment to mission.* Here the disciples find their place in the Great Commission. They demonstrate this when they

1. Know that God has a specific mission for every believer and that it is the responsibility of believers to participate in the Great Commission.

2. Know that all acts of service must be motivated by knowledge of and love for God and must be guided and empowered by the Holy Spirit.
3. Are burdened for the salvation of the lost and seek opportunities to participate in the Great Commission.

Disciple—The Verb

A community that encourages and supports disciples is essential. The church's responsibility is to facilitate the disciples' progress through the stages of spiritual development. This means the church community must provide opportunities for the people to make the right decisions and to participate in the disciple-making process. The church must commit to the people and their spiritual development.

If we are asking people to make specific commitments essential to true discipleship, then we must help the people make and keep their commitments. The church and its leaders must make the four commitments *to include, to instruct, to involve,* and *to invest* people so they become believers, then disciples, then workers and leaders.

In our model, the church's commitments are defined by the base paths. From home plate to Base 1, the first commitment the church makes is to *include people.* At this point, the church reaches out to disciples-to-be and seeks to win them for Christ. Strategies include the more visible events of the church's life, such as the worship service, evangelistic activities, and concerts; and less visible activities, such as small-group Bible studies and fellowship groups.

Related to people's decision to accept Christ is their commitment to membership in the local church. This is an accountable relationship, which does not necessarily include the signing of a membership card. Again the church must respond with the appropriate ministry. This can include adult fellowship groups, youth and children's activities, music and drama activities, and sports teams. These ministries assimilate people into the life of the church and bond them to the local body through the relationships they make. The disciple-making process has begun.

The church can better fulfill its commitment to disciples if it develops four habits to include people by (1) ministering to their needs, (2) building relationships with them, (3) including them in groups, and (4) sharing the gospel with them. When the church develops these four habits, people are better able to make and keep their commitment to membership.

What happens to those we win through our outreaches? Do they continue to grow as mature disciples of Jesus Christ or does their spiritual development stall? Do some drop out of the game?

The answer to what happens to converts depends on how effectively we have moved the disciples from Base 1 to Base 2. The second commitment the church makes is to *instruct them.* The church's role is to establish people in the Word and to help them develop a prayer life, the disciplines and character of true disciples.

Commitment to instruct is the intensive care and development of new believers and the lifelong development of growing and mature believers. Spiritual growth is a lifelong process in gaining a more complete understanding of the principles of God's Word and making appropriate application in life.

Many believers never get beyond Base 1. Although some have been believers for many years, they have never grown spiritually. They have become socialized disciples in that they have learned to look like disciples, but the habits of true disciples are not present and consistent in their lives. They are not spiritual disciples, practicing the basic disciplines of prayer, Bible study, witnessing, and obedience.

The church that is not able to move people beyond the Base 1 of commitment to Christ faces a problem when someone is needed for a ministry or leadership role. When people on Base 1 are used, they produce the same level of disciples as they are themselves.

The church can better fulfill its commitment to instruct if it develops the four habits of (1) enrolling people in a discipleship group, (2) teaching spiritual disciplines, (3) establishing mentoring relationships, and (4) modeling a biblical lifestyle. As the church develops these four habits and keeps its commitment to instruct, the people are better able to make and keep their commitment to maturity.

To move developing disciples from Base 2 to Base 3, the church must make a commitment to *involve them*. Here the church helps people discover and develop their ministry gifts and talents. The church provides training and opportunities for appropriate levels of hands-on ministry, usually under the tutelage of a mentor.

Just as Jesus took His disciples apart and demonstrated true ministry, so the church should strive to provide a similar strategy of ministry development. Disciples develop through teaching, observing, and doing.

The church helps people understand ministry gifts and how God intends their use in specific ministry. It seeks to help people discover their gifts by encouraging their participation in a small group that cultivates their development in spiritual maturity and emphasizes reproduction of disciples.

Many people have never discovered their calling and spiritual gifts for ministry. The church is committed to helping people find the joy and fulfillment that comes from developing and using their unique God-given gifts and talents. It seeks to find ministry areas that match their giftedness. Then it continues their ministry and leadership development through ongoing training, discipling, and accountability.

The church keeps its commitment to involve people by developing the four habits of (1) identifying ministry gifts, (2) establishing ministry apprenticeship, (3) providing leadership training, and (4) modeling servant character.

The fourth commitment of the church is to *invest disciples*. The ultimate role of the church is to invest them in Great Commission service. Disciples are equipped and mobilized to find their place in Kingdom ministry. This may include a greater role of leadership within the local body or ministry that goes beyond the church walls. In our definition people truly become disciples who disciple others.

As people are discipled, develop the basic habits, and begin to discover and develop their gifts, they are put to work. The primary focus of this stage of development is ministry. The plan is for people to invest themselves in the Kingdom, reproducing the life and character of Christ in the lives of others so that they too will go and make disciples. Some who move to this base in the process may move on to other ministries, such as missions, helping to start a new church, developing a new ministry, or just being more effective in their places of employment so that God is truly glorified.

The church's commitment is to invest in the lives of people, then invest them in the kingdom business of Christ. Ministry roles at this stage include special interest and outreach groups, where disciples serve in key ministry or leadership roles. Ministry teams, mission teams, marketplace and service groups all provide opportunities for people to use their gifts in ministry and leadership.

The church keeps its commitment to invest by developing and maintaining the four habits of providing (1) cross-cultural experiences, (2) leadership experiences, (3) opportunities to disciple others, and (4) continued leadership training.

Summary

True disciples make commitments in these four areas: membership, maturity, ministry, and mission.

The model of the bases helps us see more clearly the decisions disciples make. Using the bases as touchstones, we can determine where people are in their spiritual development and what the church must do to help them progress farther.

The church assumes responsibility to win and disciple people by its commitment to include, to instruct, to involve and to invest them. People are won through the church's outreach and they grow into mature disciples who will then disciple others. The church fulfills its commitment by providing a community that includes people in the church's life, instructs them in the spiritual disciplines, involves them in ministry within the body, and eventually invests them in the broader church mission.

Consider the following important questions:

1. Where am I in my development as a disciple? What decisions do I need to make to progress farther?
2. How effective is my church as a disciple-making community? What strategies do we need to initiate?

---

[1]Edythe Draper, *Draper's Book of Quotations* (Wheaton, Ill.: Tyndale House Publishers, 1992), 335.

[2]*Disciple,* Vote Sunday School Convention, Fort Worth, Tex., 1993.

4
The Law of Inclusion

A church's effectiveness in evangelism-disciple making is directly proportional to its ability to establish and cultivate meaningful relationships.

The success of a church is measured by the people it reaches and helps to be conformed to the image of Christ, not by the number of its programs. If people do not connect through a relationship with Jesus Christ, all the other ministries will eventually stop happening. God depends on His people, the Church, to get most of His kingdom work done. Herb Miller says, "No Christian people—no Christian service. No evangelism—no missions accomplished. The pastor-people ministry team in a vital congregation, therefore, adopts attitudes and enacts methods that encourage people outside the church to experience a life-changing connection with Jesus Christ."[1]

The disciple-making church includes people so they can find a life-changing relationship with Christ and His body.

The Law of Inclusion Defined

The Law of Inclusion says: A disciple-making church intentionally provides a process that includes people in its sphere of care, causing them to desire to become believers, establishing a relationship with Jesus Christ and His body, the local church. They make a commitment to membership.

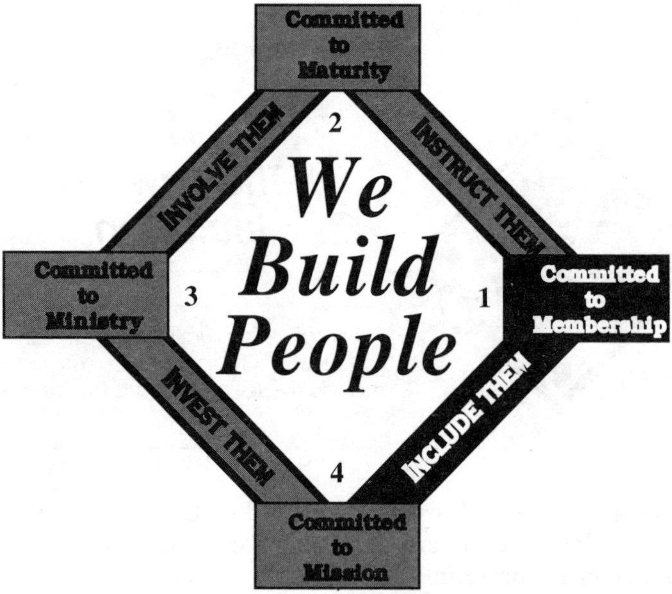

The Law of Inclusion is the first commitment that the church makes to people so they might enter into a meaningful, eternally significant relationship with Jesus Christ and His body, a local church.

Churches frequently suffer from "I" problems. Their ministries and activities are focused primarily on their own members. Churches that practice the Law of Inclusion include the unchurched, hurting, searching, and nonbeliever in their circle of love. The objective is to reach lost people for Jesus Christ, helping them to become active and responsible members in the body of Christ.

Unhealthy churches have barriers that keep them from including people. Signs that barriers may exist include (1) more thinking about the past than planning for the future, (2) more emphasis on maintaining programs than on ministering to people, (3) few programs or ministries that intentionally and effectively reach out to the unchurched, (4) many newcomers feeling they don't fit or belong, (5) a large percentage of guests not returning, (6) evangelism being nonexistent or becoming a forced program that demands great energy and produces little results.

A commitment to include starts with a genuine compassion for lost people and a deep commitment to the Great Commission.

The commitment to include people in our circle of care is fueled by the conviction that every person has a right to a presentation of the gospel at his or her level of understanding and by these three supporting principles: (1) The timeless message of the Bible is the answer to human need (Psalm 19:8). (2) The priority of Christ and His church is the salvation of each individual (Matthew 28:19,20; Luke 19:10). (3) We influence first by our character and caring, then by what we communicate (Mark 6:34).

The Law of Inclusion Modeled

Jesus reached out to the multitudes at their point of need. He healed them. He fed them. He touched them. He included them through love and compassion, addressing the hunger and the hurt in their hearts and lives.

Jesus called His first disciples to "come and see" His life, character, and compassion (John 1:39, KJV). The lifestyles of church members must reflect the values, principles, and character of Christ.

People's lives are significantly influenced when they are included in the circle of love and care of a Christian or a group of believers. Jesus modeled the priorities of a disciple-making church by (1) reaching out to people where they were, (2) ministering to and caring for people at their point of need, (3) teaching people biblical truths and principles through example and words, (4) including people in relationships and activities, (5) leading people to a spiritual new birth.

Most churches have this order backward. They try to evangelize people before they have included them in their circle of care. Effective churches (1) reach out to people, (2) minister to their needs, (3) teach them the power of biblical truth and principles in everyday life and issues, (4) establish credible relationships with them, (5) then lead them to a personal relationship with Christ.

Effective churches intentionally design the disciple-making process to lead people to make a commitment to membership by including them in loving relationships and caring ministry.

Commitment to Membership Explained

In the model, Base 1 is a commitment to *membership,* a personal relationship with Jesus Christ and with His body, a local group of believers. Salvation is the first decision a person must make to become a disciple.

Two destructive myths have infected and weakened the church. The first myth is that by merely saying a prayer one becomes a Christian. The act of going forward to pray after a sermon or praying a simple prayer with the host of a Christian TV program doesn't necessarily make one a Christian. Responding emotionally to a sermon is not the same as repenting of sin. A person becomes a Christian only through repentance, being sorry for and turning from sin. Jesus said, "'No one can see the kingdom of God unless he is born again'" (John 3:3).

True conversion begins with God's work of regeneration in our lives. It is instant the moment we repent and is progressive as we continue to grow in faith. Those who say a prayer at the altar and are told they are now Christians—without true repentance—have not experienced conversion. The result is that they have no desire or power to live above sin, no hunger for truth and holy living, and no sorrow or remorse for sin.

The second prominent myth that has infected the church is the belief that people can be Christians apart from the church.

The church is God's plan, not man's. Attempting to develop their own unique belief system, placing themselves at the center of their own personalized brand of Christianity is both arrogant and destructive. God called people to live in community with and accountability to other believers. Norman Kraus says, "Mankind's sin is not the assertion of individuality in community, but the assertion of individual independence and self-sufficiency from God and his fellows."[2]

Jesus reinforced this principle of community. He spent more time preparing the community of His 12 disciples than He did proclaiming the good news. He was not training them to be individuals; He was training them to be His body, interdependent and working together in the context of the group. This is the power of a community committed to God and to each other.

The Book of Acts reveals the normal pattern of community. Each believer made a public confession of faith, was baptized in water, and became accountable to a local body of believers. This is a commitment to membership. They became members in the universal Church through salvation and in the local church through accountability.

Membership is fundamental to faithful Christian life. It is not an option for a true disciple. Failing to become accountable to a local church is in direct defiance of the biblical warning not to forsake assembling together (Hebrews 10:25). John Calvin said, "He cannot have God for his Father who owns not the church for his mother."[3]

Being a member of a church does not bring salvation, but one cannot fulfill what it means to be a Christian apart from the church. Signing a membership card is not as important as establishing an accountable relationship with a local church, the body of Christ.

In a community of believers people grow, develop, and fulfill God's design for their lives. The first step after receiving Christ as Savior, becoming part of the universal Church, is to become accountable to the body of Christ, a local church. This is a commitment to membership.

Four Habits of Disciple-Making Churches

The church cannot call people to commit themselves to membership if it doesn't provide the means to fulfill it. The church's responsibility is to provide an environment and process that includes the unchurched and nonbelievers in its sphere of care and ministry, causing them to desire to make a commitment to membership.

Four habits characterize the church committed to include people and to act on its conviction.

Minister to Needs

Churches that include people develop the habit of ministering to people's needs. Churches can do several things to develop this habit.

Understand the People We Are Trying To Reach

George G. Hunter III discusses in more detail the general characteristics of the people the church is striving to reach today. Here is an overview of those characteristics.[4]

They are essentially ignorant of basic Christianity. Most people don't know the basics of the Bible or the purpose of Christianity. They are ignorant of Christian values, Bible stories or references, and traditional Christian culture.

They are seeking life before death. People fear extinction more than they fear hell or seek heaven. They are more concerned about life before death than life after death. They struggle to find meaning, purpose, significance, and to make a difference in this life.

They are conscious of doubt more than guilt. Guilt is viewed as a social problem but not a personal problem. People who feel guilty are more inclined to see a therapist to learn to deal with their guilt than to see a minister to find spiritual help. Most people are more doubting than guilty in their own minds.

They have a negative image of the church. People doubt the intelligence, relevance, and credibility of church leaders,

Christians, and the church and its claims of truth. They view the church as out of touch and not able to deal intelligently or practically with real-life issues.

They have multiple alienations in their lives. People are alienated from their families, friends, communities, government, and nature. Many feel lonely, detached, isolated, and unloved.

They are untrusting. Broken relationships, alienation, being taken advantage of, and being manipulated lead to distrust, which creates a wall and accentuates people's sense of isolation.

They have low self-esteem. Loss of identity, worth, value, and dignity is epidemic. This leads to selfishness, self-deception, and dysfunctional behavior and relationships.

They feel the world is out of control. Assassinations, the Vietnam War, world crises, and such events were surprising and shocking. The sense that the past was out of control leads to anxiety about the future.

They feel that issues in their lives are out of control. People have issues in their families and personalities that they can't control. Addictive and abusive behavioral patterns cause many to feel that life is out of control. Their sense of hopelessness becomes self-destructive.

They cannot find "the door." People are searching for ultimate reality, life, and God, but they cannot find the door. The doors of position, power, money, alcohol, etc., all lead nowhere, increasing hopelessness.

Identify People's Needs

"Pockets of pain" exist in your church and community. Our time has become known as the Age of Rage. According to some analysts, 8 out of 10 Americans have experienced deep wounds through uncontrollable addictions, serious antisocial behavior, or some type of abuse.[5]

Identify the pockets of pain by using three methods: (1) Investigate, through interviews and surveys, the needs of people in the community and the church. Survey people who have left your church. They can give you information as to areas of pain or needs that have not been met. (2) Listen with your ears, eyes, and heart. Even individuals or families who appear to have everything together have areas of pain. Where there is pain in life, there is opportunity to minister. (3) Relate to people. Take time to develop more than a surface friendship. Build meaningful relationships, then be attentive and responsive to their needs.

Be Sensitive to Receptive Times

Naaman came to God at a time of crisis. Jesus attracted the diseased, the deluded, and the depressed. Receptivity increases during times of crisis or transition in people's lives. A few of these include the death of a family member, divorce, serious illness, abuse, birth, financial problems, job loss, a child leaving home, and a family move.

Respond to People's Needs

People's needs can be met through relationships with Christian friends, relatives, or associates who are attentive and respond to the needs.

The Sunday school class can also minister to the needs of class members' non-Christian friends. The church includes unchurched non-Christians when it ministers to them at their point of need through side-door activities or ministries, such as support groups that deal with life-controlling bondages or abuses and felt-need classes or seminars, such as the Sequence Evangelism Seminars (see resources list). Newcomers classes also can provide a way to address the needs in people's lives. The purpose is to reach people where they are and to build a bridge for them to find Jesus.

BUILD RELATIONSHIPS

The kind of relationships the church and its members have with the unchurched will determine their disciple-making ability. Building the right kind of relationships and monitoring newcomers' involvement can help develop this habit.

Build Redemptive Relationships

Build relationships with people who don't know Christ by being friendly, learning their names, and being genuinely interested in their interests. The most comfortable setting to build relationships is in the home. As the relationships develop, introduce the people to other Christians in casual settings. Be sensitive to receptive moments when you can address the deeper spiritual issues in people's lives. Be a credible friend before you try to convince people to join God's family. The church or an individual Sunday school class can help to build redemptive relationships with unchurched nonbelievers through church-sponsored activities, such as retreats, groups, banquets, etc.

Monitor People's Involvement

By monitoring four areas, you can determine if your efforts to build relationships with newcomers are effective and people are being assimilated (included and belonging) into the life of the congregation and Sunday school.

Friends: Do they have at least seven significant friendships in the church? The church must help people develop meaningful friendships.

Worship: Do they regularly attend worship services? The church must help people grow spiritually in the basic habits and disciplines of a Christian.

Role/Task: Do they have a meaningful and appropriate role or task within the church? The church must help people become involved in an appropriate and meaningful ministry role or task. Help people work together by regularly communicating the church's mission.

Group: Do they actively participate in a small-group experience? The church must help people find acceptance, belonging, nurture, and accountability in small groups.[6]

The Sunday school naturally provides one of the best structures to focus on these areas; however, it must be designed to help people in these areas. Do not assume that it will happen automatically.

Include People in Groups

Groups are the foundational component of all effective disciple-making churches. Such churches regularly start new groups and cultivate healthy group dynamics. This habit is best developed by understanding and building on the strengths of groups to reach and to assimilate people.

Groups Best Reach New People

Groups are a most effective means of evangelism and of responding to the needs and issues in people's lives. Southern Baptists have discovered the effectiveness of Bible study groups that intentionally reach out and enroll non-Christian friends, relatives, and associates of class members. They found that two out of four new enrollees are unsaved and that one out of four of those new enrollees will be saved within 12 months. One out of approximately four hundred people not enrolled in a Bible study group will be saved within the same 12-month period.[7]

New Groups Best Assimilate New People

New people who come to church will stay only if they can develop meaningful relationships with people in the church. Involving them in a group where they can develop friendships will help them grow.

New groups are more effective in assimilating new people than existing groups. Kennon Callahan in *Twelve Keys to an Effective Church* writes,

> It should be observed that new people tend to join new groups. . . . It is easier for new people to establish deeply profound relationships with one another when the network of relationships is still comparatively new, flexible, and in process for development. . . . As open and as genuinely caring as that old group seeks to be, it nevertheless takes new people a good deal of time to learn and discover their place in that already fully established network of relationships. . . . Those churches that quit starting new groups are churches that have decided to die.[8]

The addition of new groups is an essential strategy of disciple-making churches. Research reveals that if newcomers to the church are not able to develop six to seven new meaningful friendships in the church within 6 to 9 months, they are likely to leave. People who feel they fit in or belong to a small group in the church tend to remain.

Groups that reach and assimilate people have an "inclusion consciousness." They actively seek to win new people to Christ. They accept responsibility to make people feel included and at home in their group. They provide activities and opportunities for building friendships and provide ministries that address the felt and real needs in people's lives. Effective groups develop a system that involves people in caring for each other. They involve people in appropriate but meaningful ministry roles or tasks.

Share the Gospel

Our ministries are just a social gospel if we don't seek opportunities to share the true gospel. This habit is best developed if we understand how people come to Christ and we know the most effective means of sharing the gospel.

Work Through Existing Relationships

The effectiveness of our evangelism efforts is in direct proportion to the establishment and cultivation of meaningful relationships. Existing relationships are the most effective for sharing the gospel and winning people to Christ.

Networks are relationships of common kinship (the larger family), common friendship (friends and neighbors), and common associates (special interests, work relationships, and recreation) and are still the paths most people follow in becoming Christians today.

People in network relationships respond positively to the gospel and are more likely to follow as disciples because (1) network relationships provide a bridge for sharing about God's redemptive love; (2) network members are more receptive; (3) network relationships allow for unhurried and natural sharing of God's love; (4) network relationships provide natural support when the friend comes to Christ; (5) network relationships result in a church's effective assimilation of new converts; (6) network relationships tend to win entire families; (7) network relationships provide a constantly enlarging source of new contacts.[9]

Understand Stair Stepping People to Christ

A person's spiritual journey is a series of questions and awarenesses. People often come to Christ through a process of several steps.

Step 1: I doubt God's existence, the validity of the Bible, and Christianity.
Step 2: Maybe there is a God, the Bible may be valid, and Christianity may be real.
Step 3: I know there is a God.
Step 4: I know I am responsible to God for my life.
Step 5: I realize that I am a sinner and feel guilt.
Step 6: I realize that my sin has separated me from a holy God.

Step 7: I recognize that only through Jesus Christ can I be restored.
Step 8: I am willing to be saved.
Step 9: I repent of my sin and accept Jesus Christ.[10]

Train Lay Witnesses

Training people how to effectively share their faith and lead someone to a personal relationship with Christ is essential to disciple-making churches. It is also essential to the development of the Christian and to reaching non-Christian people. Many churches have used evangelism training resources, such as *Discipleship Dynamics or Evangelism Explosion.*

You can help people share their personal testimony in 3 minutes using the following three points: (1) my life before I found Christ (45 seconds), (2) my life when I found Christ (30 seconds), and (3) my life since I found Christ (1 minute 45 seconds). Encourage people to spend the most time on the third point to reinforce the fact that Christ truly makes a difference in one's life. Provide time in class for members to share their testimonies.

Training to witness can be as simple as showing people how to share the gospel using tools like the Romans Road or a tract. Intentional evangelism is always more effective than passive evangelism. It won't happen if you don't train and act.

Establish a Prayer Base

Prayer is our foundation and the power behind everything we do. Without it our ministries become stale and our efforts futile. Through prayer our plans and programs are identified and empowered. Through prayer the barriers and strongholds come down in people's lives. Praying regularly for opportunities to minister to the needs of people makes one attentive and equipped to respond. The church that prays finds the passion and power to extend a healing touch, a helping hand, and a redemptive friendship to the lost.

Designing Your Disciple-Making Process

The Law of Inclusion must be built into the values and culture of the church. It doesn't happen automatically. A church or ministry will ultimately turn inward and self-serving if steps are not taken to keep its focus on including people in its circle of care and ministry.

Base 1 ministries or activities focus on including the unchurched and leading them to make a commitment to membership (a relationship with Jesus Christ and with the local church). These ministries should focus on including unchurched nonbelievers by (1) ministering to their needs, (2) building relationships with them, (3) including them in groups, (4) and sharing the gospel with them. These are the four habits of the Disciple-Making Process (DMP) at Base 1.

Six Steps To Design Your Disciple-Making Process

This can be done for a class, ministry, or total church.

1. List each ministry or activity that enhances the disciple-making process (DMP) at Base 1.
2. Evaluate each ministry or activity on a scale of 1 to 10 as to its effectiveness and alignment with the stated purpose of Base 1 in the DMP.
3. Refocus or eliminate ministries or activities that don't enhance the effectiveness of the DMP at Base 1.
4. Identify gaps or weaknesses in your DMP at Base 1. Make sure that you are developing the four habits of the DMP.
5. Select resources and activities that can fill in the gaps and enhance the DMP at Base 1.
6. Design each ministry and activity to achieve a specific purpose in the DMP at Base 1.

Evaluating Your Inclusion Quotient (I.Q.)

The best way to determine if your church, class, or group is practicing the Law of Inclusion is to examine each individual's

I.Q. (Inclusion Quotient). Respond with a yes or no to each statement and see how you score.

1. I believe that responding to the Great Commission is the primary purpose and focus of our church and ministries.
2. I have spoken to someone in the last month about the meaning of Christ and the church in my life.
3. I have invited an unchurched friend/relative/neighbor to a church event in the last 6 months.
4. I have participated in an outreach training experience or outreach activity in the past year.
5. I have prayed specifically and regularly for the salvation of a non-Christian friend/relative/neighbor and the opportunity to share Christ with that person.
6. I have invited a non-Christian friend/relative/neighbor for a meal with the intention of building a redemptive relationship.
7. I would be willing to take a new member or guest home for dinner once every 3 months.
8. I have taken the initiative to introduce myself to a new member or guest in the past month.
9. I have taken the initiative in the last month to contact someone who has been absent from church and expressed my concern.
10. I would prefer that our pastor contact nonmembers more than members.[11]

9–10	yes	Compassionate disciple maker
7–8	yes	Concerned disciple maker
5–6	yes	Cautious disciple maker
3–4	yes	Cold disciple maker
1–2	yes	Callous disciple maker

Total all the scores to determine the I.Q. of your class, church, or leaders. What habits do you need to work on to increase your Inclusion Quotient?

Goals of Disciples Committed to Membership

How do we know when an individual has committed to membership and that the church is effectively practicing the Law of Inclusion? The person commits to Christ and to His body, the local church, and demonstrates this commitment by a change in awareness, attitude, and action. More than just acting like a disciple, the person is becoming and developing as a true disciple of Christ.

At Base 1 true disciples should reflect the following awarenesses, attitudes, and actions in their lives.

Awareness Goals

People demonstrate a commitment to membership when their *awareness* is enlightened and they know (1) what sin is and why people need a Savior; (2) that they can be saved by repenting of sin and receiving Christ as Savior and Lord; (3) that the Church is Christ's body and are compelled to fulfill the threefold mission of worship, edification, and evangelism; (4) that the Church is the family of God and that each believer is vital to the Church's mission; (5) that the Bible is the infallible, unique written revelation of God to humankind.

Attitude Goals

People demonstrate a commitment to membership when their *attitudes* reflect (1) a realization that they are sinners; (2) godly sorrow for sin and a desire to accept God's gift of salvation; (3) a desire to symbolize conversion through water baptism; (4) a recognition of the value of Christian fellowship; (5) a respect for the divinely inspired, infallible Word of God.

Action Goals

People demonstrate a commitment to membership when they take *action* and (1) come to God seeking forgiveness; (2) turn from sin in repentance; (3) testify of their conversion through water baptism; (4) consistently join the fellowship of believers; (5) use the Bible to investigate claims concerning Christian faith.

Profile of Disciples Committed to Membership

What is the profile of people committed to membership? They demonstrate the characteristics of true converts. They exhibit godly sorrow for sin; they repent and accept God's gift of salvation through Jesus Christ. They testify of conversion through water baptism and evidence new life in Christ through a change in awarenesses, attitudes, and actions (see 2 Corinthians 5:17). They show love toward Jesus and hate sin. They know the Church is the family of God and begin regularly to join the fellowship of believers. They begin to value the Bible and use it to discover principles for life and living.

The inclusion phase of your Disciple-Making Process is effective when you are developing disciples that match this profile.

Resources

The following resources, intentionally focusing on salvation, are available to guide the church in helping adults make a commitment to membership:

Special Worship/Celebration/Rally Events

Adult Sunday School Classes

Radiant Life Curriculum for adults and young adults, and the *Spiritual Discovery Series* (Gospel Publishing House)

Support Group Ministries

For couples in second marriages and blended families; for parents of difficult children; for grief recovery; Turning Point (Teen Challenge)

Divorce Recovery Workshops and Seminars (Gospel Publishing House)

God's Design for Broken Lives—Rebuilding After Divorce (02-0344)
Divorce Care video series and study materials (28-0175)

Sequence Evangelism Seminars (Sunday School Promotion and Training Department)

Learning To Love (714-409)
Closeness Through Communication (714-405)
Positive Parenting (714-408)
How To Talk So Your Teen Will Listen (714-406)
Managing Life's Stress (714-410)
Time and Priority Management (714-430)
How To Make Christianity Real (714-411)

---

[1]Herb Miller, *The Vital Congregation* (Nashville, Tenn.: Abingdon Press, 1990), 70.

[2]C. Norman Kraus, *The Authentic Witness* (Grand Rapids: William B. Eerdmans Publishing Co., 1979), 85.

[3]Gerald Tomlinson, ed., *Treasury of Religious Quotations* (Englewood Cliffs, N.J.: Prentice-Hall Publishers, 1991).

[4]Adapted from George G. Hunter III, *How To Reach Secular People* (Nashville, Tenn.: Abingdon Press, 1992), 44–54.

[5]Adapted from Robert E. Logan and Larry Short, *Mobilizing for Compassion* (Grand Rapids: Fleming H. Revell Co., 1994), 45.

[6]Adapted from Win Arn, *Basic Growth Seminar,* Pasadena, Calif., May 1983.

[7]Andy Anderson, seminar, Springfield, Mo., 1993.

[8]Kennon L. Callahan, *Twelve Keys to an Effective Church* (San Francisco: Harper and Row, Publishers, 1983), 36–37.

[9]Adapted from Win Arn, *The Master's Plan for Making Disciples* (Monrovia, Calif: Church Growth Press, 1982), 33.

[10]Adapted from Elmer Towns, *Winning the Winnable* (Lynchburg, Va.: Church Growth Institute, 1989), 17.

[11]Adapted from Arn, *The Master's Plan for Making Disciples.*

5
The Law of Instruction

The measure of a great church is seen in the quality of disciples that it makes rather than the size of the crowd it attracts!

The night before his assault on the Matterhorn, John R. Noe drifted off to sleep with the five high mountain climbing do's and don'ts playing over in his mind like a stuck recording. Do everything my guide tells me every step of the way. Place my hands and feet exactly where he places his above me. Don't give up, no matter how much it starts to hurt. Never ask the psychologically defeating question, how much farther is it? Remember all the way up that the most difficult part is the climb down.

John conquered the mountain because he had guides who taught him the principles and skills of mountain climbing. New believers, as well as more seasoned Christians, need to learn the basic principles, skills, and disciplines necessary to succeed in conquering the mountain of life.

The Law of Instruction Defined

The Law of Instruction says: A disciple-making church provides an intentional process of Bible-based, life-centered instruction that contributes to the lifelong learning and development of believers.

The Law of Instruction is the second commitment that the

church makes to develop disciples by providing sound, practical, biblical learning experiences so believers continue their spiritual development throughout life: For new believers, intensive discipling experiences so they can learn the basic disciplines, habits, and knowledge of true disciples; for more mature believers, practical learning experiences that address the everyday issues of life and deepen their relationship with God.

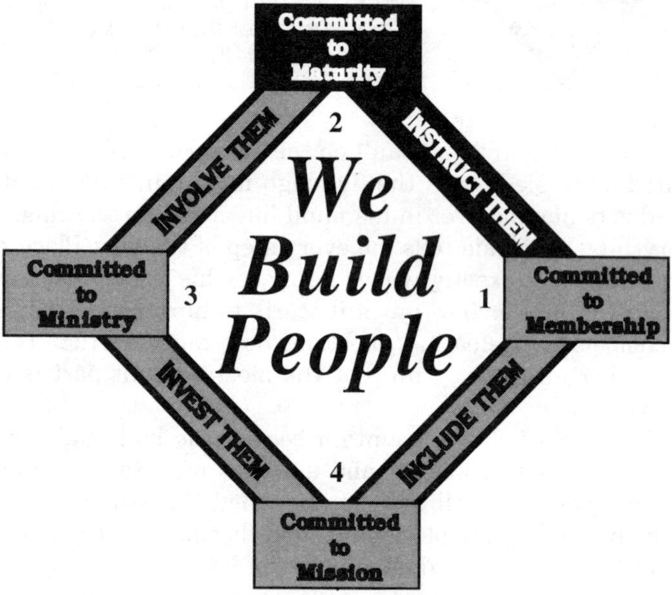

A commitment to instruct means helping believers focus on the development of the inner life, rather than external behaviors, through the development of basic spiritual habits, such as Bible study and prayer.

Many churches never develop believers beyond Base 1. People have made a decision to follow Christ but never learned the basic disciplines of Bible study, prayer, and sharing their faith. They never develop the habits of disciples. They don't know the basic tenets of faith or the basic biblical principles for Christian living.

When the church needs teachers for classes or leaders for groups, it often finds them at Base 1, which is dangerous. People must be servants before they can be leaders. People who are placed in leadership positions before they have developed the disciplines, character, and heart of true servants will never learn to be servants.

People who are placed in positions before they develop the appropriate level of spiritual maturity can become addicted to the power and prestige of their position and become self-serving, controlling, and domineering.

By placing people from Base 1 in leadership roles, the church perpetuates substandard disciple making. Leaders teach what they are, not what they know. People who are faithful but who have never learned or do not maintain the basic disciplines in their lives will build people who have the same weaknesses.

The commitment to instruct means that all leaders of the church must become proven disciples. Spiritual authority is not based upon position; it is based upon leaders modeling the church's values, Christian character, and Christian lifestyles. If leaders are not proven disciples, they cannot develop true disciples.

The commitment to instruct comes from a greater desire to develop people than to maintain programs. It starts with the conviction that all people need a biblical moral compass to guide and protect them throughout life. This conviction is upheld by the three principles that (1) personal growth is a lifelong process (1 John 3:2); (2) parents are their children's first and primary teachers (Deuteronomy 6:6–9); and (3) acceptance, caring, and learning occur best in small groups (Luke 6:13).

The discipling process must include solid doctrinal instruction. It is the core of a disciple's life and commitment. It must also include helping believers develop the disciplines and habits characteristic of strong disciples.

The Law of Instruction Modeled

When Jesus spoke to the disciples and said, "'Come, and follow me, . . . and I will make you fishers of men'" (Matthew 4:19), He was taking responsibility for the development of His disciples. They watched Him minister to people. Then He sent them back to their homes, their jobs, and their nets. Some estimate this took approximately 4 months.

Jesus had given them time to observe His character and life. He demonstrated His credibility. He proved His compassion. He inspired in them hope and a vision. He called them to commit to lifelong spiritual growth and obedience as He made this commitment to them: "I will make you fishers of men."

Jesus understood that His disciples must make a commitment to maturity, but He also had to commit to instructing and developing them.

When the disciples realized that Jesus was willing to commit to their personal development, success, and future, they were able to make their commitment. The church must also commit to the process of helping believers develop their full potential in God. This means having a plan while being sensitive to people and to their needs.

Could it be that one of the primary reasons people don't make commitments is because of our lack of commitment to them and to their personal development? Do we have a process that builds people or do we just have events and programs that people ought to attend?

"Why should I be committed to your Sunday school class or your church?" "What benefit will I gain?" "Will the benefit to my life be worth the cost?" These are the questions people ask. Jesus was committed to His disciples' spiritual success. He didn't call them to be part of His program. He wasn't just trying to increase attendance at His sermons. He was serious about helping them become everything God designed them to be. People will commit to us when they know we are committed to adding value and meaning to their lives.

Commitment to Maturity Explained

Base 2 requires a commitment to *maturity,* lifelong spiritual growth and development. Becoming a disciple does not end at the point of repentance and commitment to membership. A disciple makes a commitment to lifelong growth and development.

Maturing is the second commitment a believer must make to be a disciple. Jesus called His disciples to a relationship that was more than just going to the temple on the Sabbath or placing a gift in the offering. Jesus desired to teach them important principles and truths, to develop their character, and to build the disciplines required of a true disciple. He wanted to train them to become "self-feeding," growing Christians, to establish them in the Word, prayer, fellowship, witnessing, obedience, and love for others.

Personally knowing and experiencing God is a priority for believers who are committed to maturity. From this knowledge and experience the Holy Spirit re-creates our inner being. Our behavior is shaped by the change in values, attitudes, and motives.

It is possible never to move off of Base 1, never to mature, but that is not God's plan. William Barclay writes that "it's possible to be a follower of Jesus without being a disciple; to be a camp-follower without being a soldier of the king; to be a hanger-on in some great work without pulling one's weight."[1]

True and successful disciples maintain a learning attitude throughout their lives. They continue to evolve as disciples. They understand that what they are "becoming" is more important than what they are "doing." Throughout their lives they continue to grow in their understanding of the Word, in the development of their gifts, and in the practical application of both to the situations of life.

Four Habits of Disciple-Making Churches

To fulfill the commitment to instruct developing believers into disciples, the church must focus on four habits characteristic of effective disciple-making churches.

Enroll in a Discipleship Group

The first habit is to enroll people in a discipleship group. This is foundational to all effective discipling. Understanding the value of groups that develop people and the reason for enrolling disciples helps to reinforce this habit.

History shows that developing disciples has been most effective in group settings. John Wesley developed small group communities called societies and bands that met weekly. New and more mature believers were expected to participate. The groups were designed to help people experience and develop the spiritual disciplines of worship, prayer, confession of sin, Bible study, and accountability for Christian living.

Groups Best Nurture and Develop People

Acceptance, caring, and learning occur best in small groups. Research from the Southern Baptists found that 1 out of 5 (20 percent) people led to Christ through personal soul winning will follow through to baptism, but only 1 out of 10 (10 percent) will follow through who are won in crusades and mass evangelism outreach events. Through small group Sunday school classes, 9 out of 10 (90 percent) will follow through with their conversion experience and be baptized in water.

It is evident that when people accept Christ in the context of relationships with a Bible study group or Sunday school class, 90 percent will continue to develop as disciples and be baptized. This means that if people respond to the altar call following the pastor's message but don't have existing relationships with a group or class or don't find a group to be nurtured in, only 10 percent will follow on to develop as a disciple. Which means of evangelism is the focus of your church?

Groups Best Care for People

People hunger for someone to care. They seek acceptance and relationship. Charles Swindoll says, "The neighborhood bar is possibly the best counterfeit there is to the fellowship Christ wants to give His Church. It's an imitation, dispensing liquor instead of grace, escape rather than reality, but it is a permissive, accepting, and inclusive fellowship. It is unshockable. It is democratic. You can tell people secrets and they usually don't tell others or even want to. The bar flourishes not because most people are alcoholics, but because God has put into the human heart the desire to know and be known, to love and be loved."[2]

The church must provide the community and family that people are seeking. What about your group? Do people come because of obligation or because their needs for meaningful relationships and personal growth are being met?

The Sunday school class or Bible study group is the best place to identify and care for people's needs. If the group is larger than 12 or 15, it can be divided into care groups of 5 with a leader for each group. The care group leader role is to provide appropriate and regular contact with group members and be sensitive to their needs.

Groups Teach

A Christian's spiritual development is enhanced by being part of a healthy group that teaches biblical values—the principles of love, acceptance, and forgiveness—which brings them healing and hope.

Characteristics of a healthy group that nurtures and develops disciples include (1) close family atmosphere; (2) application of Bible principles; (3) individual care; (4) opportunities to share life's testimony; (5) encouragement and edification;

(6) opportunities for meaningful service; (7) relational evangelism; (8) intensive care and discipling of new converts; (9) spiritual growth; and (10) leadership development.

We enroll people in life-changing Bible study groups because groups are the primary environment in which nurturing and growth can occur. The group is the place to learn, develop, and practice the principles of Christian living. People need a group and accountability to help them increase in commitment and spiritual growth. In the context of the nurturing group they find and fulfill God's design for their lives; they gain a sense of belonging; and they can develop their unique identities.

The *Church Growth Spiral* is designed to help churches focus on growing people through groups by managing their groups.

Teach Spiritual Disciplines

The habit of teaching spiritual disciplines is developed through understanding the necessity of teaching spiritual disciplines, what the basics disciplines are, and how to best teach them.

Need for Teaching Spiritual Disciplines

Observing the consequences of not teaching spiritual disciplines, Ken Hemphill says, "Our failure to take seriously the teaching of basic life skills has led to spiritual impotence in the average Christian's life, and this in turn has created weak churches that have little impact on American society today."[3] Obviously the individual, the church, and our society suffers from the church's failure in this area.

Many people in our churches—some have been attending for years—have never learned the basic disciplines for Christian living. J. Robert Clinton in his book *Connecting: The Mentoring Relationships You Need To Succeed in Life* lists three reasons why discipling at this level is very appealing and also very necessary. He says:

> First of all, many people who were socialized in the last three decades suffer from a lack of discipline. These people often long for clarity and practical help in bringing about a stable, consistent growth pattern for their spiritual life.
>
> Second, many people who became followers of Christ in recent years are products of dysfunctional family situations due to the turbulent years of the sixties, the "me generation" of the seventies, and the "affluent years" of the eighties. They are willing to go through rigorous and relational discipleship programs if these will bring wholeness at the other end.
>
> Third, a well-designed discipleship experience instills a basic Christ-centered spirituality that can provide a foundation for a lifetime of following Christ. The disciplines learned and practiced will strengthen and tune the believer so he or she is quick to sense the Spirit's leading and draw upon God's grace and resources to exploit opportunities and endure hardships. It is similar to a well-trained athlete, who has far greater capacity to fully use all his talents in a challenging situation than a lesser-conditioned one with equal ability. The Apostle Paul and the writer of Hebrews often exhort us in these areas (2 Timothy 2, 1 Corinthians 9, Hebrews 5 and 12).[4]

The need and opportunity to help believers develop basic Christian disciplines is great. People are an expression of the habits in their lives, so the church must help believers know and practice the right habits; the church is only as strong as the people it develops. The following basic disciplines need to be taught and practiced.

Word: Personal reading and study of Scripture on a regular basis to hear God's voice and to gain God's perspective on life and ministry is essential. Additional insights are gained through others' teaching and preaching of the Word.

Prayer: Personal, intimate prayer with God on a regular basis is necessary so the believer can respond and draw close to Him. Intercessory prayer for the needs of others and for the church must also be learned.

Community: One must learn to see the value of a commitment to other believers and establish the habit of regularly meeting together with them. Together as followers of Christ, they commit themselves to obediently carry out His commands. This is necessary for correction, edification, encouragement, worship, and guidance.

Obedience: One must learn how to respond obediently and appropriately to God's Word and Spirit. Obedience leads to a life of holiness that pleases God.

Stewardship: One must learn to regularly commit 10 percent of personal income to the ministry of God's people—the lifestyle of generosity.

Family: One must have a regular time with spouse and children, separately and together. Give attention to matters of spiritual, emotional, and physical well-being, and give attention to family affairs, such as finances and home maintenance.

Ministry: Praying for the lost and feeling both a concern for the lost and a desire to share ones own relationship to Christ with others is essential. The believer should share with others what he or she has learned about following Christ. The believer should be involved in appropriate ministries that develop and use his unique gifts.

Keys to Teaching Basic Disciplines

Every church will have to design its own plan for teaching basic disciplines. If people are going to learn them, it will most likely happen in their spiritual infancy.

In the early stages of spiritual development, intensive care and nurture are essential. These basic skills can be taught by a personal mentor or in small groups. Cover all the habits and provide for repeated learning until the behavior becomes ingrained. "A Stanford University study revealed that it takes hearing something seven times in order to form an opinion. It takes an additional seven times to internalize what is heard. A person must hear a truth at least eleven times in order to change a false conception. Combine this finding with the results of the Princeton University study which shows that 21–28 days of doing the same thing is required to form a habit and you see the need for patient and habitual training during this developmental stage."[5]

Establish a Mentoring Relationship

Mentoring is a lost skill in the church but essential to the developing of disciples. This habit is strengthened by defining mentoring and understanding the types of mentoring relationships and the practices of effective mentors.

Mentoring Defined

A mentor is a tutor, coach, counselor, guide, and friend. One whose experiences, insights, qualities, and characteristics are transferred to someone else, facilitating the other's growth and development. Mentors are able to share in the spiritual development of people.

Mentoring is a partnership between God, other mentors, the Word, the Holy Spirit, and the mentoree. Mentors are laborers together with God. Paul described the mentoring partnership, saying, "I planted the seed, Apollos watered it, but God made it grow" (1 Corinthians 3:6).

Characteristics of a Good Mentor

Jesus demonstrated six characteristics of a good mentor. (1) He could see through the roughness of an individual and detect potential. (2) He showed tolerance with the disciples' mistakes, faults, abrasiveness, and such in order to fully develop their potential. (3) He was not rigid in His schedule or goals but showed flexibility in responding to people in varying circumstances. (4) He was patient with the disciples, knowing that time and experience are needed for development. He did not expect them to be perfect. (5) He had the vision and ability to see the future and to guide the disciples to the next step in their growth. (6) He used His gifts and abilities to build up and encourage the disciples.

The result of Jesus' mentoring was that the disciples turned the world right side up. Their influence is still active in the world. What could happen if each leader would mentor one person the way Jesus mentored the disciples? We can change the world if we do our part and remember that Christ is our partner in the process.

Model a Biblical Lifestyle

The closer that the values, character, and lifestyles of members align with biblical Christian living, the greater the positive influence members have on each other and on their community. Leaders, individual members, and the church as a whole increases its disciple-making effectiveness by modeling a biblical lifestyle.

Leaders Must Model

Christ is our model. As leaders involved in ministry, our values and lifestyles must reflect those of Christ. We are models for those we serve.

The apostle Paul said, "Even though you have ten thousand guardians in Christ, you do not have many fathers, for in Christ Jesus I became your father through the gospel. Therefore I urge you to imitate me. For this reason I am sending to you Timothy, my son whom I love, who is faithful in the Lord. He will remind you of my way of life in Christ Jesus, which agrees with what I teach everywhere in every church" (1 Corinthians 4:15–17).

What do those who are influenced by us learn about how to handle adversity, crisis, conflict, or irritations? What qualities do they see in our lives that they should emulate? Do the lessons our lives teach strengthen people's faith, build up the church, or lead people to the light? It has been said, "No matter what you teach the child, he insists on behaving like his parents." That is the power of our lives as models.

The Church Must Model

Each of us teach good or bad lessons through our actions. We influence our families, those who love and admire us, coworkers, and even strangers.

Believers were to show the power of Christ's redemption in their own lives by exemplary conduct in every area of life (Romans 12:1 to 13:7; Colossians 3:12 to 4:1). The Christians were expected to adopt a new lifestyle appropriate to their commitment to Christ (Ephesians 4:17–24). The overcoming of sins in the lives of Christians was a witness to the redeeming power of Christ in action in the church community (Galatians 5:22–26), and the sins to which the communities were prone were identified and challenged (5:19–21).

The way members of the church were to treat one another was modeled by what God had done in Christ for the church. They were to forgive one another (Colossians 3:12–14) and to love one another (Ephesians 5:1,2; 1 John 3:16) because God had done this for them in Christ, thus the declaration of Jesus, "'By this all men will know that you are my disciples, if you love one another'" (John 13:35).

As the church cooperates with God's purposes in restoring relationships in the church, it demonstrates God's love and power to a lost and searching world.

Designing Your Disciple-Making Process

The Law of Instruction must be built into the values and culture of the church. It doesn't automatically happen. A church or ministry will become weak, unstable, and ineffective if disciples are not trained in, and practicing, the basic disciplines of Christian living.

Base 2 ministries or activities focus on instructing and nurturing new believers in the foundations of faith and practice and on maturing believers throughout life by the continued integration of truth with life and service. The goal is that believers will make a "commitment to maturity" (lifelong spiritual growth and development). We want every believer to "grow in the grace and knowledge of our Lord and Savior Jesus Christ" (2 Peter 3:18) and that in all areas of our lives we "grow up into [Christ] who is the Head" (Ephesians 4:15).

The ministries at Base 2 need to focus on (1) enrolling all

believers in a discipleship group; (2) teaching spiritual disciplines; (3) establishing mentoring relationships for spiritual growth and development; and (4) modeling a biblical lifestyle. These four habits of the Disciple-Making Process (DMP) at Base 2 help people make and fulfill their commitment to ministry.

Six Steps To Design Your Disciple-Making Process

This can be done for a class, ministry, or the total church.

1. List each ministry or activity that enhances the disciple-making process (DMP) at Base 2.
2. Evaluate each ministry or activity on a scale of 1 to 10 as to its effectiveness and alignment with the stated purpose of Base 2 in the DMP.
3. Refocus or eliminate ministries or activities that don't enhance the effectiveness of the DMP at Base 2.
4. Identify gaps or weaknesses in your DMP at Base 2. Make sure you are developing the four habits of the DMP.
5. Select resources and activities that can fill in the gaps and enhance the DMP at Base 2.
6. Design each ministry and activity to achieve a specific purpose in the DMP at Base 2. Designing the church, class, or group to fulfill the Law of Instruction means focusing on proven habits of effective disciple-making churches and making sure that everything we do is done to build people.

Evaluating Your Instruction Quotient (I.Q.)

The best way to determine if your church is practicing the Law of Instruction is to examine each individual's I.Q. (Instruction Quotient). Respond with yes or no to each statement on the test to see your score.

1. I believe that developing people is the primary focus in our church and ministries.

2. I regularly and systematically pray, read, and study my Bible.
3. I enrolled one person who did not attend a Sunday school class or Bible study group in the past 6 months.
4. I intentionally focused on spiritually mentoring one person in the past year.
5. I demonstrate my commitment to maturity by being involved in a weekly Bible study group.
6. I shared my faith with one person in the past 3 months.
7. I tithe 10 percent of my income to God through the local church.
8. I am accountable to an individual or small group for my lifestyle and spiritual growth.
9. I believe the values, character, and lifestyles of our church members reflect that of Christ.
10. I believe people can follow my example and please God in their lives.

9–10	yes	Serious discipler
7–8	yes	Sacrificing discipler
5–6	yes	Supporting discipler
3–4	yes	Sad discipler
1–2	yes	Sterile discipler

Total all your scores to determine the I.Q. of your class, church, or leaders. What habits do you need to work on to increase your Instruction Quotient?

Goals of Disciples Committed to Maturity

How do we know when the individual has committed to maturity and that the church is effectively practicing the Law of Instruction?

These believers will commit to a process of lifelong spiritual growth and development. As a result, their whole life, awarenesses, attitudes, and actions will be elevated to a higher spiritual plane.

At Base 2 true disciples reflect the following growth in their awareness, attitudes, and actions.

Awareness Goals

People demonstrate a commitment to maturity when their *awareness* is enlightened and they (1) know the baptism in the Holy Spirit is for all believers, bringing a supernatural power for life as a witness; (2) know that Christlikeness is the aim of the Christian life; (3) know that loving God is the primary directive of the disciple's life; (4) know that loving God is evidenced by our love for others; and (5) know the biblical principles and commands that provide guidance in matters of faith and conduct.

Attitude Goals

People demonstrate a commitment to maturity by reflecting an *attitude* that (1) desires the baptism in the Holy Spirit; (2) desires to live a Christlike life; (3) desires to love God fully and completely; (4) is concerned with the spiritual and physical needs of others; and (5) desires to live by biblical principles and commands.

Action Goals

People demonstrate a commitment to maturity when they take *action* and (1) enter into a Spirit-filled life by seeking and receiving the baptism in the Holy Spirit; (2) make the principles and commands of the Bible the ruling factor in all decisions; (3) develop a consistent pattern of corporate and personal prayer and worship; (4) respond to the spiritual and physical needs of others; and (5) study the Bible in a regular and systematic manner.

Profile of Disciples Committed to Maturity

What is the profile of disciples committed to maturity? They demonstrate characteristics of growing disciples. As followers of Jesus Christ, they put Christ first in all areas of their lives. They take steps to live separated from sin and dedicated to God (Luke 9:23; Romans 12:1,2). They grow in the Word through regular systematic Bible study and Scripture memorization. They make the principles and commands of the Bible the ruling factor in all decisions. They consistently apply the Word to their lives with the help of the Holy Spirit (Psalm 119:59; John 8:31; James 1:22–25). They maintain a consistent devotional life and are growing in faith, character, and intercessory prayer (Mark 1:35; Colossians 4:2–4; Hebrews 11:6). They enter into a Spirit-filled life by seeking and receiving the baptism in the Holy Spirit. They attend church regularly and show Christ's love by identifying with and serving other believers (Psalm 122:1; John 13:34,35; Galatians 5:13; Hebrews 10:25; 1 John 4:20,21). They openly identify with Jesus Christ where they live and work, manifest a heart for witnessing, give their testimony clearly, and present the gospel regularly with increasing effectiveness (Matthew 5:16; Colossians 4:6; 1 Peter 3:15). As disciples they are open and teachable. They are visible followers and learners of Jesus Christ and demonstrate consistency and faithfulness in all of the above areas.

In John 15:7–16 Jesus reveals four characteristics of disciples committed to maturity. (1) They are loyal. They remain in Christ and consistently live to become more like Christ. (2) They are obedient to Christ and accountable to His body, a local church. (3) They produce spiritual fruit in and through their lives. (4) They bring honor and glory to God through their lifestyles, character, and values.

The best evidence that the instruction phase of your Disciple-Making Process is effective is when you see believers' lives reflecting the goals of those committed to maturity.

Resources

Some of the resources available from Gospel Publishing House to help the church lead adults to make a commitment to membership are listed here. These are resources and activities that intentionally focus on helping believers develop the values, character, and lifestyles of true disciples.

Adult Sunday School Classes

Radiant Life Curriculum for adults and young adults and the *Spiritual Discovery Series*

New Believers/Discipleship Classes and Home Bible Studies

Beating Mediocrity, by John Guest (03-1109)
Your New Life in Christ, by Michael Clarensau (02-0766)
Pentecostal Experience: The Writings of Donald Gee, ed. David Womack (02-0454)

---

[1]*Biblical Illustrator* [online], Parsons Technology, 1993.

[2]Charles R. Swindoll, *Dropping Your Guard* (Waco, Tex.: Word Books, 1983), 128.

[3]Ken Hemphill, *The Antioch Effect* (Nashville, Tenn.: Broadman & Holman, 1994), 196.

[4]Paul D. Stanley, *Connecting: The Mentoring Relationships You Need To Succeed in Life* (Colorado Springs, Colo.: NavPress, 1992), 50–51.

[5]Hemphill, *The Antioch Effect,* 196.

6
The Law of Involvement

To the extent that a church develops its most appreciable asset, people, it will succeed at accomplishing its part in the Great Commission.

Several years ago, a 94-year-old widow died. She was known as an antique collector. An astonishing collection of things were found in her estate: a collection of chinaware, paintings, and unopened trunks. It was reported that 20 rooms were packed with rare furnishings, diamonds, $5,000 in cash, and many uncashed checks and money orders.

We consider ourselves experts in the care of what we call valuables—the people God has placed in our churches—yet we fail to use them properly, leaving the God-given gifts in people's lives undiscovered and undeveloped."

The Law of Involvement Defined

The Law of Involvement says: A disciple-making church provides a process that intentionally involves disciples in identifying and developing their unique God-given gifts, abilities, and resources.

The Law of Involvement is the third commitment the church makes to people to help them develop and fulfill God's purpose for their lives.

The church's commitment to involve people means moving

people from the spectator to participant in ministry, doing ministry with them rather than doing ministry for them. Bill Hull emphasizes this point, saying, "The more we ask people to come and sit and listen to us talk, the greater the disservice we do to them and to Christ's commands."[1]

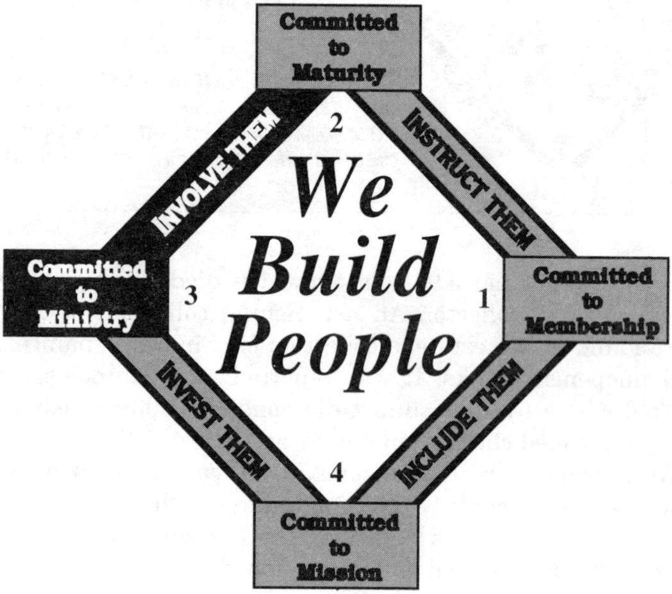

The commitment to involve means reestablishing the biblical role of leadership to equip people for ministry. The equipping church intentionally devises a process to fulfill the mandate in Ephesians 4:12,13: "Prepare God's people for works of service, so that the body of Christ may be built up until we all reach unity in the faith and in the knowledge of the Son of God and become mature, attaining to the whole measure of the fullness of Christ."

In the effective disciple-making church, ideally, the pastor will spend 80 percent of his time training and equipping 20 percent who are workers and leaders. The remaining 80 percent are equipped to do ministry as workers. Everyone is serving and is being ministered to.

A commitment to involve means realizing that the greatest asset in the church is the talents and resources of its people. The church must take seriously its responsibility and commitment to prepare God's people for works of service and ministry. To fulfill this commitment, the church must be united in the purpose of reaching and developing people. They must help people discover and develop their gifts, then release them to serve in the reaching and developing of other people.

Organizations ultimately die when they fail to develop the human talent, energy, and resources. Thomas Jefferson said in his *Notes on Virginia,* "We hope to avail the nation of those talents which nature has sown as liberally among the poor as the rich, but which perish without use, if not sought for and cultivated."[2]

The commitment to involve people means equipping people, helping them identify and develop their unique gifts and abilities.

The commitment to involve starts with the conviction that every believer has unique gifts to be developed and used to strengthen the church. It is further strengthened by three supporting principles: (1) Obedience is the essence of discipleship and the highest form of worship (John 14:23); (2) Responsibility for equipping the believer is vested in the church (Ephesians 4:11–13); (3) Biblical leadership requires servanthood and godly character, as well as ministry skills (Mark 10:42–44).

The Law of Involvement Modeled

Jesus worked with His disciples as they made the second major decision, a commitment to maturity. He now called them to make a commitment to ministry, to come and be with Him

(Mark 3:13–15). He wanted to develop their unique gifts and skills for ministry, to show them how to minister, and to minister with them. He wanted to involve them in ministry at appropriate levels based on their growth and maturity as apprentices.

Jesus knew that people are born with unique God-given abilities and skills to be identified, developed, and dedicated to God for His purposes.

Commitment to Ministry Explained

Base 3 requires a commitment to *ministry,* to identify and develop people's unique gifts, abilities, and resources for God.

This is the third commitment believers must make to become disciples. They cannot achieve God's purpose for their lives without committing themselves to discovering and developing their unique, God-given gifts and abilities.

The priorities for disciples' lives at Base 3 is first of all training for ministry, then worship, Bible study group, and ministry involvement.

A striking feature of the Early Church is that every member of the church had a gift for service that was to be used cooperatively for the benefit of all (Romans 12:1–8; 1 Peter 4:10). Paul used the imagery of the human body to illustrate this unique feature, stressing that all Christians have a responsibility to operate with an awareness of their share in the body of Christ (1 Corinthians 12:12–31).

A commitment to ministry was expected from believers in the Early Church. They realized they couldn't fulfill God's design and purpose without discovering and developing their place in the body of Christ.

In the Parable of the Talents, Jesus taught that people are counted faithful by using what they have been given (see Matthew 25). God does not consider the amount of people's talent but the development and use of their talent.

When Jesus calls people to a commitment to ministry, He intends for them to develop to their full potential. The church is responsible to continue developing them in works of ministry and service.

Four Habits of Disciple-Making Churches

Identify Ministry Gifts

The habit of identifying ministry gifts is strengthened by accepting the theology of gifts and ministry, evaluating the ministry climate in your church or class, determining ministry needs in the church, and helping people discover their place in ministry.

Theology of Ministry Gifts

The Scriptures are clear about each person's role in ministry and that each person is provided with specific gifts to use for God's purposes. Several observations can be made from Scripture.

1. Each member has received gifts from God (1 Corinthians 12; Romans 12).
2. Each member is responsible to use his or her gifts for God (1 Peter 4:10).
3. Each member has a unique God-given mission that only he or she can perform (Romans 12:4,5).
4. The gifts are nontransferable (Romans 12:6).
5. The effectiveness of ministry increases when the gifts are used for God (1 Corinthians 12).
6. Christ has declared that all believers are a part of the royal priesthood (1 Peter 2:9).
7. Ministry is the responsibility of all believers (1 Peter 4:10).
8. There are differences in ministry but not in value (1 Corinthians 12:12).
9. The priesthood is called to proclaim, teach, worship, love, witness, and serve (1 Peter 2:9,12).
10. The role of ordained ministers is to equip and mobilize believers for ministry (Ephesians 4:11–13).

Volunteer Ministry Climate

What is the volunteer environment in your congregation? It is often difficult to involve people in ministry because the ministry climate is not healthy. Take time to complete the following sentences. Ask people in your class or group to respond to the questions, or hand out a questionnaire for a more accurate evaluation of the volunteer ministry climate of your church.

1. People volunteer to work in our church because:
2. People don't volunteer in our church because:
3. Some things that turn off volunteers in our church are:
4. People feel good about volunteering in our church when:
5. We could increase the number of volunteers by:
6. We could increase the quality of volunteer ministry by:

Discovering Their Place in Ministry

Help people discover their place in ministry in these five ways:

(1) Identify passion. Passion is an intense God-given desire to give ourselves to a cause, vision, idea, people, or ministry for an extended period of time. What is the burning desire in their hearts? What things really bring them the greatest sense of fulfillment? What do they do very well? What are their dreams for making a difference?

(2) Understand personal temperament. This will help them understand themselves and the others they relate to in life and ministry. Resources are available to help people understand temperament or behavioral style.[3]

(3) Identify ministry gifts. This can be done through prayer or a Bible study on spiritual gifts (Romans 12; 1 Corinthians 12). Have them identify personal desires, evaluate using a spiritual gifts inventory, experiment with ministries, identify what brings the greatest fulfillment, seek confirmation from other people, and evaluate where they get the best results in ministry. Resources include the Spiritual Gifts Inventory.

Other gifts assessments are also available. (See the list at the end of this chapter.)

(4) Identify skill strengths. People tend to relate better in life with either their hands, doing; their heart, feeling/sensing; or their head, thinking. Natural skill strengths tend to lie in one of these areas and can be identified best through experiences.

(5) Confirmation from the group. People around us often see our areas of strength better than we do. They will confirm with honest appreciation and genuine recognition of our ability in areas of strength.

Resources that can help the church develop a ministry for gifts discovery and placement strategy are listed at the end of this chapter.

Establish Ministry Apprenticeship

The habit of establishing ministry apprenticeship is strengthened by understanding the nature of apprenticeship training, the process of leadership development, and how to establish a ministry apprenticeship strategy.

Apprenticeship Training

The advantage is that this training provides real-life situations in a relational setting with the mentoring leader as a model. The strength of apprentice training depends on the ability of the mentor-leader who must first be a good model, be able to assess and challenge the trainees growth, then be able to teach at teachable moments. The apprentice experiences limited leadership opportunities. The real learning for the apprentice takes place in the planning and evaluation times with the mentor-leader, who will talk through the process of identifying individual and group needs, explaining behaviors, and addressing questions.

Leadership Development Process

Leaders are developed slowly through a partnership with the individual, the workings of God, and the church.

J. Robert Clinton in his book *The Making of a Leader* has identified and defined six phases in the development of an individual life for ministry.

Phase 1 is sovereign foundations. God is establishing the foundation for the individual life. God is working providentially through the person's environment, family, culture, and experiences from birth. The primary objective is to learn to respond in a positive way to the uncontrollable issues of life—trusting God.

Phase 2 is inner life growth. God is working to develop the inner life of character and obedience. Through trials and tests God desires to teach foundational lessons as well as help one begin to discover his God-given gifts. The person should learn how to pray and to hear from God. Discernment, understanding, and obedience are the primary objectives at this point.

Phase 3 is ministry maturing. The individual experiments with various ministry opportunities, gaining some understanding about personal spiritual gifts. God is developing the person through ministry and relational experiences, positive and negative, within the body of Christ. Ministry development is the primary objective.

Phase 4 is life maturing. God begins to work through the person, who has discovered and has begun using ministry gifts in ministry. The person finds a greater sense of fulfillment. In learning what to do or not do, in keeping with God's unique gifts in and design for one's life, the person finds increased effectiveness in ministry. The primary objective is to learn to respond to the experiences God allows and to deepen communion with God.

Phase 5 is convergence. God shifts the person into a role that matches one's gifts and experiences. Life maturity and ministry maturity converge, thus maximizing the person's ministry effectiveness. The major objective is to trust, rest, and watch.

Phase 6 is afterglow. All the fruit of a life of faithful ministry and growth are rewarded with respect, recognition, and influence. Few people ever reach this phase.[4]

Apprenticeship Strategy

Leadership development is not a mystery. Include people in decision making. Delegate, giving them responsibility and authority. Stretch and challenge them. Periodically change their assignments. An effective apprenticeship process can be developed following these six steps:

Analyze: Determine gifting, abilities, interests, passion, personality, commitment, energy, and time available.

Assign: Give specific task assignments that are challenging, yet attainable. Design the level of difficulty around the team members' skills and experience. Think through the progression of tasks you assign to ensure that the level of challenge steadily and consistently increases.

Coach: Provide vision, adequate resources, and consistent support for your team members to stand on as they seek to achieve each task.

Evaluate: Schedule regular reviews in which to evaluate experiences, summarize results, and discern areas for improvement.

Praise: Acknowledge your team members' unique contributions; affirm their intrinsic value to the team; and celebrate all victories.

Promote: Create and provide continuing opportunities for personal and professional growth, renewal, and challenge.

PROVIDE LEADERSHIP TRAINING

The habit of providing leadership training is best developed by understanding the principles, processes, and practices of leadership training.

Principles of Leadership Training

Several principles can help guide you as you develop leaders.

1. Focus training to influence both character and conduct.
2. Adapt your style and methods of equipping to the students' characteristics, circumstances, and needs.
3. Master the basics before attempting to develop advanced skills.
4. Encourage students more frequently during early training.
5. Train until students have successfully mastered the skill and can function independently.
6. Focus more intensely on those most committed.
7. Motivate with meaningful relationship, recognition, and reward.
8. Realize that training is most effective when it includes both teaching and practice.
9. Affirm the students' value independent of their performance level.

Processes of Leadership Training

Here is a partial list of processes that can be used to train leaders and equip them for ministry.

Training events, such as workshops and lab experiences, are usually one-time events that focus on developing specific skills, techniques, or awareness. Choose a skilled trainer or teacher in a specific area of expertise to help in the training. These experiences are more effective if they are combined with opportunities to practice the skills or use the information being taught.

Training courses may last over a period of time and require regular commitment and participation. They tend to focus on communication of information but should include experience opportunities. The training is more effective if the participants have opportunity to practice what they have learned in the groups where they minister.

Conference or retreat experiences provide concentrated training to develop skills or communicate ideas in a relational setting and offer a great opportunity for team building, inspiration, and motivation.

Apprenticeship training provides training in real-time and real-life situations in a relational setting. A weakness is having a weak mentor.

Existing groups and committees provide settings for equipping in group dynamics and leadership skills. Some instruction and training can come through observation and debriefing.

Practices of Leadership Training

Training is the key to unlock the potential of people. Since people are the greatest resource to any organization, training them is the key to unleashing the potential of the organization. Several principles can help any leader develop the people he serves.

Train individuals, not the masses. Each individual has a different personality, learning style, and rate of learning. If you focus on training the individual, you can use different approaches to training and be sensitive to the needs, temperaments, and styles of each person.

Reinforce the basics. Everyone needs to know the basics of the game, the game plan, and the plays. Organizations often fail because they forget to reinforce the basics.

Use teachable moments. Take advantage of teachable moments in an experience or circumstance to teach and train. Don't get trapped into thinking that training is imparting knowledge. Training is most effective when the theory and the practice are closely connected.

Tie training to personal benefits. People are more motivated to learn when they know how they will be benefited by it. Any training plan needs to answer three questions for the trainee: What benefit is this training to me? How will my competence be increased? In what way is this training relevant to me, my life, my job, or my ministry?

Provide on-the-job training. Provide opportunities for people to practice and develop in the areas of ministry for which they are being trained. Practice increases people's confidence and competence and provides teachable moments as they face issues that were not totally addressed in the teaching sessions. These times increase their desire to learn.

Use short training sessions. Take advantage of brief but effective opportunities for training in formal and in informal settings. A good formula is Knowledge + Study + Practice = Competence/Quality.[5]

Model Servant Character

To model servant character requires that leaders know the qualities of servant-leaders, possess servant character, and be able to distinguish the difference between God's way and man's way of leadership.

God's Way versus Man's Way of Leadership

Man's way of leadership is to focus on power, freedom, personal gain, immediate fulfillment, praise of men, being served, self-gratification, ambition, leadership, and competition.

God's way of leadership is to focus on submission, responsibility, giving, lasting achievement, approval of God, serving others, self-control, patience, following God, and cooperation.

Jesus drew the distinction between the hireling and the shepherd. The characteristics of the shepherd and God's way of leadership speak of the servant-leader; the characteristics of the hireling and man's way of leadership represent the nonservant leader (John 10).

Qualities of Servant-Leaders

Isaiah 42:1–5 lists the primary characteristics of servant-leaders. The passage speaks of Jesus, the true servant-leader.

These characteristics should be evident in our lives if we are models of servant character.

Voluntary dependence. "Here is my servant, whom I uphold" (v. 1). Jesus was totally dependent upon His Heavenly Father. Even though He had power and abilities, He yielded them to be used as His Father willed. He submitted to the leadership and authority of God.

Divine approval. "My chosen one in whom I delight" (v. 1). Jesus received divine approval because of His obedience to God's divine plan for His life and submission to God's authority. In Psalm 40:8, another Messianic passage, Jesus says, "I delight to do Thy will, O my God" (NASB). Divine approval comes by delighting in God's will.

Divine anointing. "I will put my Spirit on him" (v. 1). The touch of God upon His life and ministry made Jesus effective and influential. Charisma is the result of one touched by God's grace. Servant-leaders seek God, then minister out of God's abundant grace imparted to their lives. Supernatural results can come only when our natural man is touched by God's grace and anointing.

Meek spirit. "He will not shout or cry out, or raise his voice in the streets" (v. 2). God's servant would not be cheapened by loud, flamboyant, self-centered ministry. Jesus was modest and meek. He demonstrated quiet confidence and could not be tempted with position, power, or prestige. A true servant does not draw attention to himself or seek personal gain through position or power.

Empathetic compassion. "A bruised reed he will not break, and a smoldering wick he will not snuff out" (v. 3). Jesus was compassion in action—sensitive and empathetic to the weak, poor, and hurting. He gave himself to the down-and-outers and the up-and-overs alike.

Faithful optimism. "In faithfulness he will bring forth justice; he will not falter or be discouraged till he establishes justice on earth" (vv. 3,4). Jesus had a mission. He would remain faithful until the purpose had been accomplished. Servants face discouragement and frustration like anybody else, but they are different in that they remain faithful.

Championing justice. "In faithfulness he will bring forth justice; he will not falter or be discouraged till he establishes justice on earth" (vv. 3,4). Jesus knew justice will again reign on this earth. He faithfully lived right and sought to restore righteousness to people and to the world.

Inspiring hope. "In his law the islands will put their hope" (v. 4). Jesus brought hope to people. He inspired with His life. He was credible. They believed in Him and His Word. He was honest. They knew He had their best interest in mind, which inspired hope in them. Hope is both a characteristic and a result of a true servant-leader.

A. W. Tozer sums up this issue of servant leadership. "A true and safe leader is likely to be one who has no desire to lead, but is forced into a position of leadership by the inward pressure of the Holy Spirit and the press of the external situation. Such were Moses and David and the Old Testament prophets. . . . The true leader will have no desire to lord it over God's heritage, but will be humble, gentle, self-sacrificing and altogether as ready to follow as to lead, when the Spirit makes it clear that a wiser and more gifted man than himself has appeared."[6]

Modeling servant character means being a servant at the core of our lives, not just trying to act like a servant. Only then is servant character modeled; only then are people equipped.

Designing Your Disciple-Making Process

The Law of Involvement must be built into the mentality and culture of the church. It doesn't automatically happen.

Base 3 ministries focus on leading believers to make a commitment to ministry, to identify and develop their unique gifts, skills, and abilities. These ministries should be focused toward involving believers by (1) helping them identify their ministry gifts, (2) establishing ministry apprenticeship with them, (3) providing leadership training for them, (4) and modeling servant character before them. These are the four habits of the Disciple-Making Process (DMP) at Base 3 to help people make and fulfill their commitment to ministry.

Six Steps To Design Your Disciple-Making Process

This can be done for a class, ministry, or total church.

1. List each ministry that enhances the disciple-making process (DMP) at Base 3.
2. Evaluate each ministry on a scale of 1 to 10 as to its effectiveness and alignment with the stated purpose of Base 3 in the DMP.
3. Refocus or eliminate ministries that don't enhance the effectiveness of the DMP at Base 3.
4. Identify gaps or weaknesses in your DMP at Base 3. Make sure you are developing the four habits of the DMP.
5. Select resources and activities that can fill in the gaps and enhance the DMP at Base 3.
6. Design each ministry and activity to achieve a specific purpose in the DMP at Base 3.

Designing the church, class, or group to fulfill the Law of Involvement means focusing on proven habits of effective disciple-making churches. It means making sure that everything is done for the purpose of developing disciples into equipped Christian workers.

Evaluating Your Involvement Quotient (I.Q.)

The best way to determine if your church is practicing the Law of Involvement is to examine each individual's I.Q. (Involvement Quotient). Respond with a yes or no to each statement to see how you score.

1. I believe that equipping people for ministry according to Ephesians 4:11–13 is regularly happening in our church.

2. I believe that equipping people for ministry is a primary focus of all those in ministry in our church.
3. I have helped someone in the past year to discover his calling and spiritual gifts for ministry.
4. I have participated in the training of one person for ministry in the past year.
5. I have completed three or more training experiences (course, conference, seminar) this past year.
6. I have helped one person in the past year find a ministry area that matches his or her giftedness.
7. I pray regularly that God will send laborers.
8. Our staff and layleaders involve large numbers of people in ministry rather than doing everything themselves.
9. I have expressed my appreciation to or rewarded someone serving with me in the last 3 months.
10. Our church has an intentional strategy that helps members identify, develop, and use their gifts for God in ministry.

9–10	yes	Powerful equipper
7–8	yes	Passionate equipper
5–6	yes	Passive equipper
3–4	yes	Poor equipper
1–2	yes	Pathetic equipper

Total all your scores to determine the I.Q of your class, church, or leaders. What habits do you need to work on to increase your Involvement Quotient?

Goals of Disciples Committed to Ministry

The way people are evaluated ultimately shapes who they become.

A church that is practicing the Law of Involvement will result in believers making a commitment to ministry.

These believers will commit themselves to discovering and developing their unique talents, gifts, and resources. As a result, their lives, awarenesses, attitudes, and actions will be heightened.

At Base 3 true disciples should reflect the following growth in their awareness, attitudes, and actions.

Awareness Goals

People demonstrate a commitment to ministry when their *awareness* is enlightened and they (1) recognize that love of God requires service to others; (2) know that greatness is measured by servanthood; (3) know the church cannot function without the participation of each believer; (4) know that each believer has been gifted for service; (5) know that Christian service is done more effectively through united rather than individual efforts.

Attitude Goals

People demonstrate a commitment to ministry through *attitudes* that (1) desire to serve Christ by involvement in ministry opportunities; (2) exhibit a spirit of humility and teachability in the service of others; (3) desire to love God by serving others; (4) recognize accountability as stewards; (5) appreciate the opportunities of service the local church provides.

Action Goals

People demonstrate a commitment to ministry when they take *action* and (1) identify their spiritual gifts for ministry; (2) develop gifts through guided ministry; (3) seek to serve the church after the pattern of Christ; (4) model godly character that influences others toward Christian maturity; (5) contribute time, talent, and material possessions to the ministry efforts of the local church.

Profile of Disciples Committed to Ministry

Disciples committed to ministry demonstrate characteristics of workers and true servants. They demonstrate growth in the virtues and skills outlined under the profile of disciples committed to maturity (1 Peter 3:18). They exhibit a servant's spirit of humility, faithfulness, and teachability in service to others. They desire to serve Christ by involvement in ministry opportunities. They recognize and accept their responsibility and accountability as stewards, contributing time, talent, and material possessions to the ministry efforts of the local church. They develop their unique gifts through guided ministry involvement and training opportunities, seek to serve the church after the pattern of Christ, and model godly character that influences others toward Christian maturity. They show a growing compassion for the lost and demonstrate their ability to lead people to Christ personally (Matthew 9:36–38; Romans 1:6). They are used of God to establish believers who have become disciples, either personally or in a discipling group context (Colossians 1:28,29). They are currently engaged in the task of making disciples (Matthew 28:19). Regular intake of God's Word and a personal quiet time are now habits in their lives.

You know the involvement phase of your Disciple-Making Process is effective when you see believers' lives reflecting the goals and profile of a those committed to ministry.

Resources

The following resources and activities that help maturing disciples identify and develop their unique gifts, resources, and skills to fulfill God's purposes through their lives are available to help the church lead adults to make a commitment to ministry.

ACTS Seminars and Workshops (Sunday School Promotion and Training Department)

(Sample Topics)

WS45—*Helping Adults in Crisis*
WS49—*Understanding Leadership Styles*
WS57—*How Do I Fan the Flame Without Burning Out?*

WS60—*Discovery and Development of Gifts / Abilities; Where Do I Fit In?*
WS76—*Welcoming Visitors and Incorporating Newcomers to the Adult Class*
WS77—*A Closer Look at Middle-Aged Adults*
WS86—*Breathe New Life Through Leadership Development*

Spiritual Gifts Identification Class

Spiritual Gifts Discovery and Implementation Guide, or *Unleash Your Church!* (Mobilizing Spiritual Gifts Series), by Paul Ford and Pat Springle (available from Fuller Seminary Press, 84 N. Robles Avenue, Pasadena, Calif. 91101)
Team Ministry Manual—A Guide to Spiritual Gifts and Lay Involvement, by Larry Gilbert (available from Church Growth Institute, PO Box 7000, Forest, Va. 24551)
Spiritual Gifts Inventory (available from Church Growth Institute, PO Box 7000, Forest, Va. 24551)

Sunday School Teacher Training & Specialization Courses (Gospel Publishing House)

Focus on Adults—A Handbook for Teachers (02-0407)
Our Church in Ministry (02-0608)
Knowing Your Bible (02-0352)
Understanding Bible Doctrine (02-0353)
Your Sunday School at Work (02-0341)
Mastering the Methods (02-0340)

Leadership & Discipleship Classes (available from Gospel Publishing House)

Developing the Leader Within You, by John C. Maxwell (03-1290)
Lifestyle Discipleship, by Jim Petersen (03-1892)
Inside the Mind of Unchurched Harry and Mary, by Lee Strobel (03-1861)

Berean study courses (Berean University, 1475 N. Campbell Avenue, Springfield, Mo. 65802)

Adult Ministry Training and Opportunities (available from the Sunday School Promotion and Training Department)

Marriage & Family Life Ministries Leadership Manual (714-424)
Single Adult Ministries Leader's Guide (714-417)
Senior Adult Ministries Packet (714-422)
Men's Ministries
Women's Ministries
Adult Choirs
Orchestras

---

[1]Bill Hull, *The Disciple Making Church* (Old Tappan, N.J.: Fleming H. Revell Co., 1990), 129.

[2]John Gardner, *John Gardner on Leadership* (New York: Free Press, 1990), 74.

[3]For example: Ken Voges and Ron Braund, *Understanding How Others Misunderstand You* (Chicago: Moody Press, 1994), or Bob Phillips, *The Delicate Art of Dancing With Porcupines* (Ventura, Calif.: Regal Books, 1989).

[4]Adapted from J. Robert Clinton, *The Making of a Leader* (Colorado Springs, Colo.: NavPress, 1988), 43–47.

[5]Adapted from Sheila Bethel Murray, *Making a Difference: 12 Qualities That Make You a Leader* (New York: Berkley Books, 1990), 228–33.

[6]Hans Finzel, *The Top Ten Mistakes Leaders Make* (Wheaton, Ill.: Victor Books, 1994), 31.

7
The Law of Investment

The size of a leader is determined by the depth of his convictions, the height of his ambitions, the breath of his vision, and the reach of his love.

—D. N. Jackson

In Paris after World War II, Abbe Pierre, a Catholic friar, was assigned to work among the beggars. He decided to show them how to mobilize themselves. First, he taught them to do their tasks better. Next, he led them to build a warehouse and start a business. Finally, he inspired the beggars by giving them responsibility to help a beggar poorer than themselves. The project really succeeded.

After years of this work, no beggars remained in that French city. Pierre believed his organization was about to face a serious crisis. "If I don't find people worse off than my beggars, this movement could turn inward. They'll become a powerful, rich organization and the whole spiritual impact will be lost! They'll have no one to serve."

This is the Law of Investment in action. The church faces a great crisis if it doesn't invest in its members, then release them to invest themselves in ministry to others.

Law of Investment Defined

The Law of Investment says: A disciple-making church provides an intentional process that releases disciples to invest themselves in the global mission of Christ and the Church.

The Law of Investment is the fourth commitment the local

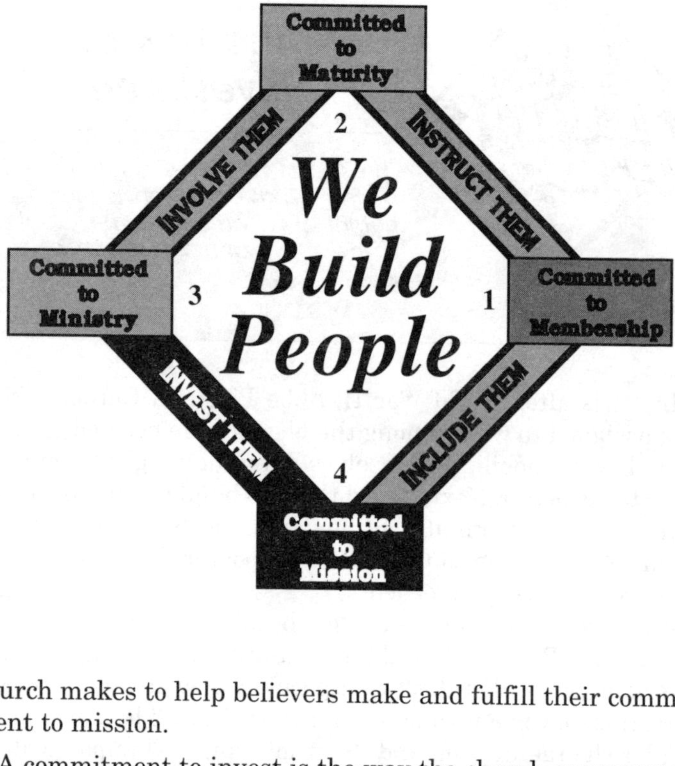

church makes to help believers make and fulfill their commitment to mission.

A commitment to invest is the way the church expresses its commitment to reproduce. Through the development of believers and disciples and the unleashing of their God-given gifts, resources, and energies, the church is able to fulfill the Great Commission. The passion of God's heart is making and developing disciples.

A commitment to invest means empowering people and ministries, releasing them for appropriate levels of ministry based upon their spiritual development. Fears may keep a church and its leaders from being able to commit to investing in people.

Some fear they will get hurt if they release and invest people in ministry. But only by investing in people and releasing them into ministry and leadership do they produce eternal results.

Some leaders fear they will lose their position or power by investing in and releasing people for ministry. They are insecure in their own abilities and position in Christ or want everything done their own way.

Other leaders fear they will lose their identity and significance by turning ministry over to others. Ministering, counseling, helping, and serving feeds their egos.

Two questions God might ask leaders and churches on the final exam are, "How many of your members are released in ministry?" and "Do their ministries result in the spiritual growth of faith, knowledge, and maturity in the lives they touch?"

A commitment to invest people in the global mission of Christ and the Church starts with the conviction that every believer has a purpose in advancing the global mission of the church of Jesus Christ. This conviction is enhanced by three supporting principles: (1) Every believer is commissioned by God to make disciples (Mark 16:15,16); (2) Spirit baptism is a priority for Great Commission service (Acts 1:4,5); (3) An awareness of need is the primary motivation for Great Commission service (John 4:35–38).

The Law of Investment Modeled

Jesus called His disciples to a life of investment. They were to remain in Him and to "go and make disciples" (Matthew 28:19). They were to continue to develop in their character and relationship with Him. They were to invest themselves in His highest purpose: making disciples. He was releasing them for leadership and ministry to reproduce in others what He had done in their lives.

Jesus had invested himself in His disciples. His ministry had been primarily focused on developing 12 men. The ultimate act of commitment came as He invested the future of the Church into their hands.

We are here today because of Jesus' commitment to invest himself in people. His influence continues 2,000 years later. Christ's influence through us will continue far beyond us if we invest in and release people for ministry.

Commitment to Mission Explained

Base 4 is a commitment to *mission,* giving oneself to advancing God's universal kingdom and the specific mission of the local church. It is giving one's time, energies, and talents to be used for God and His purpose. It is living with the reality that all the blessings, resources, and talents we have been given are to be invested in His kingdom.

People cannot call themselves true disciples of Christ if they are not giving themselves to His mission. God has a high purpose for our lives. Our individual purposes are linked to His greater purpose. Self-centeredness and an independent spirit undermine commitment to mission.

Confusing good with right also undermines our commitment to mission. As "the good" is the enemy of "the best," so "the good thing" is the enemy of "the right thing." Many people in ministry are pursuing ministry goals, projects, and programs they have adopted from another person's vision.

Trapped by the expectations of others, people live to please everyone except God. However, the only measure of success is to find God's purpose for our lives and commit to doing it!

Contrary to popular opinion, there is no success apart from fulfilling God's mission for our lives. True disciples committed to mission measure success not by what they have done compared to what others have done, but by what they have done compared to what they were supposed to do. Success is defined by purpose and measured by obedience. This is the mark of disciples committed to mission.

Four Habits of Disciple-Making Churches

Provide Cross-Cultural Experiences

The habit of providing cross-cultural experiences can be developed by understanding the value of and opportunities for such experiences.

Value of Cross-Cultural Experiences

Cross-cultural ministry experiences have the power to open people's hearts and eyes to the needs of the world. It can help people gain a passion for the lost and increase their level of commitment to God. Often it is a catalyst in motivating people to grow in character and ministry. This habit can be strengthened by identifying cross-cultural ministry opportunities.

Lives and commitments are significantly changed by understanding people's needs and experiencing God's power working through them in ministry to those needs. The greatest joy and fulfillment is in helping others find Christ as their personal Savior.

Opportunities for Cross-Cultural Experiences

A church can provide opportunities for cross-cultural experiences without going to a third-world country. Set up opportunities for ministry in the inner city or other pockets of less privileged cultures or communities. The ministry experience should extend for at least several days to a few weeks. Some churches take groups from their church to the inner city and become "homeless" for a night, walking the streets and seeing and experiencing the homeless life.

To help your group feel needs without leaving home, divide them into five groups. Blindfold one group. Tell the second group that they can't talk. Tie the hands behind the backs of the third group. Provide earplugs for the fourth group. Provide wheelchairs for the fifth group, and tell them that if they get out they can't use their legs.

After the experience ask what it might be like for people who have to live this way. What are their struggles? What must they feel? How can they best be helped?

Provide short-term cross-cultural ministry opportunities for your people. Consider encouraging each member to take 1 or 2 weeks of vacation every 3 to 4 years and go on a cross-cultural mission trip. This could be to work in the inner cities of America or to go to a foreign country. These experiences will prove to be life changing for most.

Provide Leadership Experiences

The habit of providing leadership experiences can be developed by providing a healthy team environment.

A Healthy Team Environment

Healthy team environment is where people feel included, valued, encouraged, and supported. This is the best environment in which to provide leadership experience.

1. Strive to create a climate in the church that promotes trust, openness, honesty, shared feelings, and mutual respect.
2. Develop a system of communication that provides for the sharing of relevant, helpful, timely information with the people.
3. Encourage problem-solving and decision-making opportunities by the people responsible for the ministry.
4. Give authority and responsibility in ministry roles based on knowledge and ability.
5. Work together as leaders and workers in the development of plans, creating a sense of ownership for the goals and results.
6. Encourage workers to participate in ministry-related

problem solving and decision making, to develop self-direction and self-control.
7. Emphasize the necessity of conflict resolution, collaboration, and win-win approaches to disagreements.
8. Provide a reward system that recognizes both the achievement of the church or ministry goals and the development of its members.

This type of church or class environment encourages participation and assists the ongoing development of leaders and potential leaders. People learn to be leaders best in an environment of compassion and acceptance.

Encourage people to become everything they were created to be. That is the way to build up people and develop leaders.

Provide Opportunities To Disciple Others

To encourage people to commit themselves to mission, the church or leaders need to provide opportunities for disciples to minister to others. This habit can be cultivated by developing a discipling mentality and by identifying discipling opportunities.

Discipling Mentality

As a church, determine to invest people in discipling opportunities. Involve people in levels of ministry appropriate to their training and spiritual development. A discipling mentality can be developed with four steps.

1. *Challenge* people with the vision of the church, the opportunities for ministry, and the benefits to them and others. People need to understand how the ministry fits into the purposes of the church and how their contributions make a difference.

2. *Orient* people to the ministry opportunities. Specifically focus on their choice of ministry. Help them learn the basic skills and demands of the ministry opportunity. Entry-level

ministries, such as ushers, greeters, choir, or drama require little more than basic training and faithful participation.

3. *Involve* people in discipling opportunities. People who are involved in discipling opportunities tend to grow themselves.

4. *Coach* people. As they minister through sharing their faith, nurturing a new believer, or counseling someone, they often realize what they don't know and begin to look for answers themselves. They are motivated to learn by realizing what they need to know.

Discipling Opportunities

Other ministry opportunities to consider include:

1. Crisis Hot Lines—targeted toward runaways, crisis pregnancies, suicide, drug abuse, etc., usually operate 24 hours a day, with calls directed into the homes of trained volunteers. Support ministries, such as counseling or support groups, may also be added.
2. Computer Literacy—training for underprivileged people to help them get better jobs.
3. Adult Victims of Child Abuse—support groups.
4. AIDS Ministries and Hospices—serve to meet physical, emotional, and spiritual needs.
5. Divorce Recovery Ministries—offer financial, emotional, and spiritual support.
6. Disability Ministry—compassionate ministry to those who are disabled, mentally or physically.
7. Elderly Ministries—caring visitation, helping with basic care needs, Bible studies, outings, etc.
8. Foster Homes—providing safe, stable, and compassionate homes for children.
9. Employment Ministries—care and compassion for nearly 10 percent of the workforce.
10. Shelter Homes—help, assistance, and spiritual guidance at shelters for abused and battered women, crisis pregnancies, etc.
11. Substance Abuse—support groups for substance abusers,

for codependent people, and for children and spouses of substance abusers.

12. Hospice Care—ministry to the terminally ill who need care, friendship, and compassion.

Provide Continued Leadership Training

Developing the habit of providing continued leadership training is essential for people in ministry positions. The church must continue to invest in their lives through ongoing training in spiritual growth and personal and skill development.

Leadership development is a lifetime process that occurs through interaction between one's spiritual life, natural abilities, experiences, and opportunities.

This habit is better developed by understanding various methods of continued leadership training and knowing the skills areas and topics that need continual reinforcement.

Principles of Ongoing Leadership Training

Ongoing training is essential to the growth and development of people and to the effectiveness of the ministries of the church. Following are several principles for ongoing leadership training.

1. *Ongoing leadership development comes by giving freedom to fail.* Disciples learn by trial and error—we desire to avoid failure, setting a standard of personal holiness, but we must not be afraid of failure. Peter's denial of Christ and subsequent restoration helps us realize that Christ anticipates failure and looks beyond it. The key is our attitude—in humility we recognize that failure can and may come at any time. Controlling our thoughts and disciplining our minds keeps us alert to the possibility of failure. Failures can be mistakes or sins or both. If we make a mistake, we recognize it quickly and correct the perceptions, conditions, and actions that led to the mistake. If we sin, we repent quickly and apply 1 John 1:9 (confession to God) and James 5:16 (transparency before our fellow believers

and confession to them), not forgetting the role of restorative prayer.

2. *Leadership development requires empowering.* Christ sent out His disciples to do ministry, expressing His confidence in them. Pastors should equip others, not just do the work themselves. Likewise, the goal of ministry leaders/trainers/mentors should be to equip the disciple to do the ministry and to supervise as it is done.

3. *Releasing leaders in ministry encourages growth.* After modeling appropriate behaviors, Christ gave basic instructions, then sent the 72 out to heal and cast out demons. But He always debriefed them afterward. He took advantage either of their frustration (when they were at a point of need) or their exultation (when they were excited and He really had their attention) to drive home His points. What does this mean for our training? It must be hands-on training. Because people learn by doing ministry, we shouldn't make it too easy for them or rescue them from potential learning experiences. We work with them to help them understand the goal and then model or teach some possible methods, letting them work out their own methodology for achieving the goal.

Methods of Ongoing Leadership Training

Providing ongoing leadership training can be done in a variety of methods. The best approach is what is right for the person at the time.

1. *Mentoring.* Successful teams are those in which the loss of any one individual is minimized by the fact that the individual has been training a second individual to take his or her place in just such an eventuality. Team members should understand that it is their responsibility to be both apprentice and mentor; every person should be actively involved in two training relationships simultaneously.

2. *Storytelling.* An important role of the mentor is to be a teacher. Christ sometimes would teach the crowds, but His parable was aimed at His disciples who were listening.

Afterward He would debrief them and give them the keys for understanding the parable if they needed them. Christ always sought to link spiritual truths with real-life metaphors the people would understand. This means we must understand and take into account the lifestyles of those we mentor. In mentoring an autoworker, we might want to teach about discipling in the language of quality control.

3. *Modeling.* Christ modeled appropriate behaviors before His disciples. He watched for opportunities to model key values. He would model an action, then take them aside and explain its significance, exhorting them to do likewise. A good modeling scheme is (1) both of us go out together on an activity. You watch while I do, then we debrief. (2) We do the activity together, then debrief. (3) I watch while you do, then evaluate. (4) You go out by yourself and do the activity. When you come back, we discuss.

4. *Celebrating.* Landmarks are victories and accomplishments. They provide opportunities to evaluate progress and design the next phase of growth. A disciple will have graduated to a certain level after proving that he can do thus and thus effectively on his own. As leaders we must celebrate and affirm that graduation.[1]

Field trips and networking with other churches or leaders doing similar ministry provide great ways to develop leaders. Reassignment to other ministry opportunities also keeps the person learning and growing.

Leadership Training Skills

Leaders need to continue to develop the following skills.

1. *Personal management skills* required comprise spiritual, emotional, physical, and personal skills. Topics in this area include spiritual disciplines; time/priority management; attitudes and personal development; values, priorities, and principles; and credibility.

2. *Interpersonal relationship skills* are required to relate to and interact with people in a positive and influential manner.

Topics in this area include understanding yourself and others (temperament), communicating and listening, believing in people, and conflict resolution.

3. *Motivational leadership skills* are required to influence others positively through communicating the vision and equipping others to become all they can be. These skills can be defined as the ability to see what ought to be, the wisdom to know how to make it happen, and the faith to see it through. Topics in this area include capturing, casting, communicating, coaching, containing the vision, challenging the process, and inspiring the shared vision.

4. *Personnel equipping skills* are required to develop a team and help people develop skills that will assist them in reaching their potential and thus help the organization. Topics in this area include the how-tos of team building, mentoring, envisioning the future, enlisting others, fostering networking, and strengthening others.

5. *Organizational administrative skills* are required to organize and administrate people to work efficiently and effectively through the development and maintenance of strategy and structure. Topics in this area include the how-tos of developing a philosophy of ministry, goal setting, program development, evaluation, and problem solving.

Covering these skill areas in ongoing leadership training strategies will assure development of balanced leaders in life and ministry.

Designing Your Disciple-Making Process

The Law of Investment must become a conscious part of the church's culture. A church or ministry will turn inward, stagnate, and become self-serving if it doesn't focus on releasing equipped and empowered disciples in ministry. A church must practice the Law of Investment to fully develop disciples and thus fulfill the Great Commission.

Base 4 ministries or activities focus on investing workers in places of service that fully develop their gifts and fulfill God's design for their lives. These ministries should be designed to motivate people to make and develop their commitment to mission (investing themselves in the global mission of Christ and the mission of the local church). These ministries should be focused toward investing disciples at appropriate levels of ministry based on their spiritual development by providing (1) cross-cultural ministry experiences, (2) leadership experiences, (3) opportunities to disciple others, and (4) continued leadership training. These are the four habits of a DMP at Base 4 to help people make and fulfill their commitment to mission.

Six Steps To Design Your Disciple-Making Process

This can be done for a class, ministry, or total church.

1. List each ministry or activity that enhances the disciple-making process (DMP) at Base 4.
2. Evaluate each ministry or activity on a scale of 1 to 10 as to its effectiveness and alignment with the stated purpose of Base 4 in the DMP.
3. Refocus or eliminate ministries or activities that don't enhance the effectiveness of the DMP at Base 4.
4. Identify gaps or weaknesses in your DMP at Base 4. Make sure that you are developing the four habits of the DMP.
5. Select resources and activities that can fill in the gaps and enhance the DMP at Base 4.
6. Design each ministry and activity to achieve a specific purpose in the DMP at Base 4.

Designing the church, class, or group to fulfill the Law of Investment means focusing on proven habits of effective disciple-making churches. It means making sure that everything we do is for a purpose, developing believers and disciples into effective Christian workers and leaders.

Evaluating Your Investment Quotient (I.Q.)

The best way to determine if your church is practicing the Law of Investment is to examine each individual's I.Q. (Investment Quotient). Respond with yes or no to each statement below to see how you score.

1. I believe that the releasing of people for ministry, after they are equipped, is happening in our church.
2. I have participated in an extended cross-cultural ministry experience (several days to a few weeks) in the past 4 years.
3. I have completed at least three leadership training experiences in the past year.
4. I am involved on a regular basis in a ministry role or task.
5. I have intentionally invested myself, through apprenticeship or mentoring, in the personal or ministry development of one person in the past 6 months.
6. I have shared my faith with one person in the past month.
7. I have invited an unchurched person to come and see an activity or event (worship service, outreach seminar, outreach Bible study, etc.) in the past 3 months.
8. I participate regularly in a small group that fosters continued development toward spiritual maturity and reproduction.
9. I remain in Christ through regular Bible study, prayer, and obedience to God.
10. I have expressed my appreciation to another person serving in ministry in our church in the past 3 months.

9–10 yes	Fantastic developer
7–8 yes	Fabulous developer
5–6 yes	Fair developer
3–4 yes	Faint developer
1–2 yes	Frozen developer

Total all your scores to determine the I.Q. for your class, church, or leaders. What habits do you need to work on to increase your Investment Quotient.

Goals of Disciples Committed to Mission

A church that is practicing the Law of Investment will produce believers who are making commitments to mission.

These disciples will commit to investing themselves in the global mission of Christ and its expression through the local church. As a result, their whole lives are influenced.

At Base 4 true disciples reflect the following growth in their awareness, attitude, and action goals.

Awareness Goals

People demonstrate a commitment to mission when their *awareness* is enlightened and they (1) know God has a specific mission for every life, (2) know it is the responsibility of every believer to participate in the Great Commission, (3) know all acts of service must be motivated by a knowledge of and love for God, (4) know the heart of God is to seek and to save those who are lost, (5) know all Great Commission efforts must be conceived, guided, and empowered by the Holy Spirit.

Attitude Goals

People demonstrate a commitment to mission by reflecting an *attitude* that (1) desires to follow God's mission for their lives, (2) desires to participate in the Great Commission at every opportunity, (3) is compelled to action by a growing knowledge of and love for God, (4) is burdened for the salvation of the lost, (5) desires to be fully guided and empowered by the Holy Spirit.

Action Goals

People demonstrate a commitment to mission when they take *action* to (1) discover and begin to fulfill God's mission for their lives, (2) seek opportunities to participate in the Great Commission, (3) demonstrate a growing knowledge of and love for God, (4) participate in both personal and corporate evangelism efforts, (5) demonstrate Spirit-filled and Spirit-led lives.

Profile of Disciples Committed to Mission

What is the profile of people committed to mission? They demonstrate characteristics of a committed leader. They are equipped workers who evidence growth in the virtues and skills listed under the profile of disciples committed to ministry. They discover and begin to fulfill God's unique mission for their lives. They seek opportunities to participate in the Great Commission, demonstrate and are compelled to action by a growing knowledge of and love for God, are burdened for the salvation of the lost, and participate in both personal and corporate evangelism efforts. They demonstrate Spirit-filled and Spirit-led lives in being fully guided and empowered by the Holy Spirit in life and service. They have been used of God to help those committed to maturity become committed to ministry (2 Timothy 2:2). They are uniting and leading workers in evangelizing the lost and establishing believers (Mark 1:38). They display faithfulness and integrity in their lives and ministry (2 Timothy 2:19–21).

The church's commitment to invest in people, then releasing them to invest themselves in others, will be evident in people's lives and ministry. If you are recognizing this profile in the people to whom you minister, you know your commitment to invest is being effective.

Resources

The following resources and activities, which intentionally focus on releasing workers in ministry as effective leaders and ministers, are just some of those available to guide the church in helping adults make a commitment to mission. The resources at Base 4 should help people who are already leading and ministering to do so more effectively.

Missions Trips and Opportunities

AIM Trips
MAPS

Ministry Opportunities

Light for the Lost
Adult Sunday School Leadership
Marriage & Family Life Ministries Leadership Manual (714-424)
Single Adult Ministries Leader's Guide (714-417)
Senior Adult Ministries Packet (714-422)
Men's Ministries Leadership
Women's Ministries Leadership
Adult Choirs Leadership

Ongoing Leadership Development

ACTS Seminars and Workshops (Order from Sunday School Promotion and Training Department)

- #16: *Lessons To Learn for Adults*
- #17: *Commissioned To Care for Adults*
- #18: *Power To Plan for Adults*
- #19: *Methods To Motivate for Adults*
- #20: *Seek To Save for Adults*
- #41: *The Purpose and Scope of Adult Education*
- #42: *The Secrets of Effective Classroom Discussion*
- #43: *Transitions: Understanding Adult Life Stages*
- #44: *Marriage & Family Life Education in the Church*
- #45: *Helping Adults in Crisis*
- #76: *Welcoming Visitors and Incorporating Newcomers to the Adult Class*
- #77: *A Closer Look at Middle-Aged Adults*
- #78: *Understanding Marital Dynamics & Roles*

#79: *Effective Bible Study Methods for the Adult Teacher*
#80: *Growth Spiral in the Adult Class*
#88: *Christian Education Changes Lives*
#89: *Christian Service—a Responsibility of Every Class*

Sunday School Teacher Training and Specialization Courses (Gospel Publishing House)

Focus on Adults—A Handbook for Teachers (02-0407)
Focus on Administration—A Handbook for Leaders (02-0408)
Developing Dynamic Disciples (02-0335)
Renewing Hope (02-0327)

---

[1]Adapted from Robert E. Logan and Larry Short, *Mobilizing for Compassion* (Grand Rapids: Fleming H. Revell Co., 1994), 101–3.

8
The Teacher and the New Vision

The teacher is like the candle which lights others in consuming itself.
—Italian Proverb

The preceding seven chapters have offered a complete look at the values, principles, and processes of a new vision for discipleship in the local church. This fresh look at an ancient challenge provides a thorough strategy that permeates the entire church and the entirety of life.

The success of this vision is not in its aggregate or corporate application. Though this vision is based on principles designed to affect the full ministry of a local congregation, its success is found on a more personal level. This effort established on the priority of the individual finds its ultimate expression in the smallest part of the discipling relationship by defining and redefining the heart of the teacher.

How does this new vision reach the classroom? How should its principles influence the thinking and teaching of its leaders? While the concepts of the vision are before us, this book would be incomplete without a look at these practical questions. The answers to such questions are the core of the entire effort—the effort to build people.

Building My Thinking

It is tempting to jump headlong into a ministry venture and be immersed in activities, programs, or concepts without first considering our personal need for transformation. Yet in order to be effective in building people, the local church must find teachers who are not only willing to do the necessary things, but also willing to think according to necessary values.

Building people requires "people-building" thinking. For teachers, the starting point of implementing this vision in the classroom and in other discipling relationships is to bring our own thinking into line with the heart of the vision. For our purposes, that thinking is twofold: thinking toward the individual and thinking toward discipleship.

Think Toward the Individual

Few would argue with the key value statement introduced in chapter 1, "Every individual is valued and is the focus of our ministry," but developing such thinking is not necessarily a given. Prioritizing the individual requires thinking in terms of the individual.

For example, teachers must recognize that their Sunday morning audience of 10 is not a group of 10 but a gathering of 10 individuals with 10 different sets of needs, challenges, abilities, and attitudes. As such, every classroom activity from classroom decoration to lesson delivery must pass through an evaluation of relevance to the needs of the hearers. Questions like "How does this lesson affect Bobby?" or "How could Sarah learn this concept most easily?" replace more general thoughts that take a shotgun approach, hoping to hit a relevant target.

To think toward the individual, teachers must meet every opportunity, every idea, every activity with the growth of the individual student in focus. The assumption that what is good for the whole will be good for the individual parts impairs the effort to truly build people.

While thinking toward the individual provides a guide for evaluating tools and approaches for ministry, it also leads us to a fresh look at our understanding of ministry itself. When the class or the group is our focus, our commitment to ministry is a commitment to perform a certain function for the group.

We commit to teach or lead this band of students and fulfill the appointed role until our ability or endurance runs out.

In a people-building church, the teacher's commitment is not to the function of teaching but to the recipients of that teaching. Ephesians 4:11–13 reveals that the purpose of these ministry gifts is for developing, equipping, and edifying the individual saints. Apart from the students, the role of teacher has no significance, application, or meaning.

Such thinking provides an important and clear definition of ministry. *Ministry is a commitment to people motivated by a love for God.* In the discipling relationship, any commitment to teach that does not involve an even deeper commitment to the one(s) being taught will be inferior and ultimately counter-productive.

When Jesus spoke of leadership, His focus centered on the servant nature of true, biblical leadership (Matthew 23:11). Far too often, however, ministry opportunity and position leads the opposite direction toward pride and self-aggrandizement. How does this happen? This aberration of the intent of Christ occurs when the commitment is to the function and not to the recipient. Improved teaching abilities are spent making a better teacher rather than molding a better student.

Ministry, according to the pattern of Jesus, is *a commitment to people.* It is not an ability to display the demeanor of humility in our teaching task, but a willingness to serve the needs and spiritual growth of the recipient even after the teaching task is through. Secular leadership focuses on mastery of function. Spiritual leadership trains its scope on a commitment to people.

Consider this scenario which often occurs in the local church. An individual agrees to fill a classroom teaching vacancy. A few months filled with lesson preparing and dispensing pass until the new teacher chooses to resign this ministry. Another individual is sought to fill the gap and the former teacher is relieved of discipling the class. Was the teacher committed to the function of teaching or to people?

Jesus used the sheep-shepherd relationship to illustrate

this focus on the individual. While many points can be gained from this analogy, one fact is clear: The shepherd was committed to the sheep. His quality as a shepherd was measured not by the size of the flock, but by his commitment to each of his sheep.

Ministry is not only a commitment to people, it is a commitment motivated by a love for God. In John 21, Peter is asked three times by Jesus, "Do you love me?" Christ told him, "'*Feed my sheep!*'" (John 21:17). Jesus directs Peter in his ministry as shepherd based on Peter's proclamation of his love for Christ. In essence, Jesus is allowing Peter to express love for Him through commitment to Christ's lambs. This is the motive we are consistently given in Scripture: Jesus says, "'If you love me . . . '" (John 14:15).

A people-building church can be identified by the people-building thinking of its people, particularly its teachers and leaders. These teachers think concerning the individual and make their commitment to the people they are called to serve.

Think Toward Discipleship

The second arena of "new" thinking in a people-building church involves the priority of discipleship. In chapter 3 we considered both the call of discipleship and the commitment a church must make to accomplish this eternal task.

First, teachers who think toward discipleship recognize that they serve God by serving people. Without the people, the church has no function.

Second, teachers accept the personal responsibility to disciple people. Discipleship is often much more involved than just classroom teaching. It involves a commitment to the individual for assistance in the full range of life-changing growth in Christ.

Third, a people-building church has teachers who judge their success by the spiritual development and values of their people. Success is not in technique or popularity, but in the evidence of "fruit" developed in the lives of the students. As students grow in maturity and ministry, the teachers see the evidence of their effort.

Fourth, such teachers recognize that their influence is built by their character and their caring more than by their abilities or creativity.

Finally, thinking toward discipleship culminates in the realization that the teachers' effectiveness is found in their own practice of biblical principles and personal growth as disciples of Jesus Christ.

This, then, is the thinking of a people builder. The individual is the target and discipleship is the goal.

Building My Teaching

The second element that teachers must bring to this ministry in order to see this new vision fulfilled is a renewed and perhaps rebuilt effort of teaching. Upon what do the teachers base their teaching? The twofold appeal of the individual and of discipleship must shape their effort.

Teach Toward the Individual

While we have already discussed turning thinking toward the individual, this second step brings the practical application of such thinking directly to the student. Each individual must be considered and evaluated in order to establish goals and priorities in teaching. To illustrate the point, let's take an example and see how this vision begins to function in our ministry as teachers.

Sherry has been teaching the third grade Sunday school class for nearly 8 years. One of Sherry's habits has been to focus part of her prayer time on her students. Once a quarter, Sherry prays and meditates on the growth of each student. She writes the students' names at the top of pieces of paper and lists their strengths and weaknesses. She then writes a short paragraph describing how she feels about each student. She asks God for specific direction in helping the students address their weaknesses and accentuate their strengths. She closes her prayer by asking God to strengthen her students' parents and give her the means to be a blessing to their efforts.

Teach Toward Discipleship

The second component of people-building teaching is teaching toward discipleship. The people-building teacher becomes focused more on the growth of the student than on the completion of the material.

Discipleship, by its very nature, is student centered. While to some, teaching may be viewed as content centered, discipleship goes further. A disciple is more than a cognitive learner. A disciple is one who is capable of reproducing the pattern of living in himself and in others. Discipleship, then, must be measured by the growth of the student.

Teaching toward discipleship may take many practical forms. Student involvement, daily application, and guided apprenticeship bring a different element to the classroom. Where discipleship is the target, the classroom becomes less teacher centered and a sort of "learning laboratory" is created.

In fact, *laboratory* is just the word that many use in describing Jim and Sarah's class. The middle-aged couples who attend the growing class say it's the most relevant study of the Bible they've ever been a part of. While Jim and Sarah do a good job of teaching the Bible lesson, it's the creative application time that has their students buzzing. Jim and Sarah have one guiding rule for their class. "We don't talk about anything that can't be lived," Jim explains. Bible lessons are sandwiched around panel discussions and role plays that help the students discover ways to apply the principles they're learning. "Before we leave the class, we already know a few ways to apply what we've learned," one student explains. "It has really made a difference in how I think and live."

Teaching toward discipleship is a constant reminder that there's more to teaching than just the message. Unless the corresponding action is developed in the student's life, the goal of the teaching effort has not been reached.

Unusual is the word commonly used to describe one young adult class. Though the class has a remarkable growth rate, the room isn't as full as you might think. Allison, who teaches the class with her husband, Dan, explains, "We believe a key part of discipling people is getting them involved in ministry so they can apply the principles they are learning and give expression to their love for God. So a lot of our class members are scattered throughout the church on Sunday morning, teaching classes or helping with other ministries."

In a discipleship environment the people are excited. They see the results of their participation in their own lives, and their excitement is making their churches grow.

Building My Targets

Once a teacher begins to think and teach toward the individual and think and teach toward discipleship, building people is just a matter of knowing the targets and taking the steps necessary to hit those targets. In the preceding chapters, we looked at 16 habits of people-building churches. Let's again consider those essential targets, but from the view of the people-building teacher.

First, we must emphasize one key point: If a teacher fails to build the concepts just presented—thinking and teaching toward the individual and discipleship—the list below becomes a meaningless checklist that will fall short of its intended goals. Such thinking and teaching are absolutely essential before even these key habits will build people.

Include Them

The small group is the ideal tool for building a sense of belonging in the local church. But it takes more than just enrolling people in a Sunday school class to build the sense of membership that opens doors to ministry. Unfortunately, many people who have attended Christian education classes for years have never become involved in an intentional discipleship relationship. In such cases, involvement in the small group has accomplished little of the purposes of Christ's Great Commission.

Ministering to Needs

People-building teachers target the felt needs of the students. While it is the power of God that meets the needs of our students, it is the compassion and genuine interest of the teacher in those needs that bonds the student to the teacher and opens the door for discipleship. Traditional tools, such as visitation and other efforts of individual attention, help provide answers to the question, "What does the individual believe he or she needs?"

Building Relationships

The classroom provides an ideal opportunity for establishing individual relationships. For the people-building teacher, this is essential. People feel belonging among friends, and they will respond to those they trust. A discipler doesn't lead from the classroom podium, but from an up close and personal vantage point.

The larger the class, the more difficult this aspect of including people becomes. Because it is virtually impossible for an individual to establish meaningful relationships with more than 20 people, additional people builders must be involved in the larger setting.

Including People in the Group

The large class finds another difficulty in this people-building habit. The teacher should never assume that attendance equals inclusion. Even those who already attend a class must be incorporated into a small group to build belonging. As mentioned in chapter 4, ministries that provide small-group fellowship are helpful. For the adult class of 20 or more, they are an absolute necessity.

Sharing the Gospel

Inclusion in Christ is the initial step in discipleship. People-building teachers recognize this fact and provide opportunities for individuals to take the first step toward spiritual growth. Teachers who believe the large setting (i.e. worship service or crusade) is more appropriate for evangelism should not be surprised if their students choose the same such settings for their spiritual maturity.

INSTRUCT THEM

While the Sunday school class is probably best equipped and has likely been most successful in providing instruction, we should not assume that a fresh look at the targets is unnecessary.

Enrolling in a Discipleship Group

For the teacher, this habit says more about the environment of the class than its existence. Why have your students come? What expectations have they been encouraged to bring to class?

Some teachers resist the concept of discipleship, believing their students aren't interested in an effort toward spiritual growth. While it is true that many adult Christians have been programmed to sit and listen and then leave and forget, we must ask how they came to that habit and who helped them develop it. Though a teacher-centered or curriculum-centered class may need a few weeks to adjust, the transition to a student-centered environment will prove worthy of the struggle.

Teaching Spiritual Disciplines

The very concept of discipleship is at odds with the idea that spiritual growth can be accomplished by occasional or weekly encounters with the truth of God's Word. Sunday is not enough for the disciple! Teaching efforts and lessons that can be opened, dealt with, and put to rest in a 1-hour session are not likely to bring life-change.

Students must be directed toward personal study of God's Word, prayer, witnessing, and other spiritual disciplines. But the simple command is seldom sufficient. People-building teachers give their students a reason to build such habits. Continued study or relevant assignments give meaning to the challenge of developing those habits that reinforce daily Christian living.

Modeling a Biblical Lifestyle

The people-building teacher is most effective when modeling the attitudes and behavior needing to be developed. Remember the familiar statement, "You teach what you know, but you reproduce what you are."

Establishing a Mentoring Relationship

If you had asked any of Jesus' disciples who was their leader, their response would have been obvious. He was their mentor, their teacher, their discipler. Because a teacher has built a relationship with the individual student, the doorway is open to establish a mentoring relationship. Such a relationship provides input, direction, and accountability—three necessary elements for making disciples.

The concern of the larger class is raised again. In such settings, leadership must be developed so everyone may find a mentor or encourager in his or her spiritual growth.

Involve Them

If the Sunday school classroom has been the primary avenue for instruction, then the Sunday school pulpit has probably been the primary place of involvement. Most people who have attended church for any length of time can recognize when a Sunday school superintendent is on the recruiting trail.

Recruiting is more effective when it is done by the discipler. Matching individuals with ministry opportunities should be the task of those who best know the individuals and their abilities.

Identifying Gifts

"What can I do?" Unfortunately, many Christians make their initial journey into ministry involvement according to the need of the ministry rather than the nature of their own gifts or abilities. The people-building teacher cares too much for the individual to let that happen. The worker's growth is of, at least, equal importance to the accomplishment of the particular task.

Various tools were listed in chapter 6 that can be used to help determine those places of involvement best suited to the individual.

Providing Ministry Apprenticeship

No students making their maiden voyage into ministry involvement should do so alone. Ministry experience provides opportunity for the application and cementing of learning. Such can be accomplished best by an apprenticeship. Even those most talented or naturally gifted should have the benefit of experienced guidance as they learn to minister. Developing such opportunities within the class structure can help. Pairing a student with a more experienced student can also enhance the growth as their friendship grows through the shared task.

Providing Ministry Training

If ministry involvement is an equal part of discipleship, then why can't our times of instruction be relevant to such involvement? It seems odd that students who have sat in a

Sunday school class for years feel ill-prepared to get involved in similar ministry. Look around your class. What training can you provide right here in the laboratory? Future teachers would benefit greatly from getting their first podium experience within the familiar confines of their own Sunday school class.

Modeling Servant Character

As noted previously, people builders become what they are by being committed to people. This commitment, which ultimately molds the heart of a servant, must be modeled. Training individuals by commanding them to develop servant attitudes builds only bitterness. Training by modeling and teaching commitment to people builds servanthood—the one true sign of Christlike leadership.

INVEST THEM

While the three previous sets of habits have a great deal of expression and opportunity for the teacher, this last group is typically more the realm of the entire church body. Still, teachers can involve themselves in this final stage of discipleship in significant ways.

Providing Cross-Cultural Experiences

The people-building teacher never really loses a student to other ministry settings. Genuine interest and prayer for the individuals who participate in such experiences gives the experience added significance. "If my teacher thinks this is important and beneficial, it must be!"

Providing Leadership Experiences

Growth through involvement ultimately brings the day when others can come alongside and benefit from the experience of the student. Leadership, for the people builder, is when the student begins to join the task of building others.

Providing Leadership Training

Involvement becomes investment at that moment when responsibility and vision for the ministry is passed to the student. But while ministry training has been a part of involvement, leadership training is equally essential now. People builders reproduce people builders. "Turning them loose" cannot imply "leaving them comfortless" (John 14:16).

Providing Opportunity To Disciple Others

The discipleship process comes full circle. Fully investing students in discipling others brings them to the level of service you have attained.

This is a key place where discipling outpaces the traditional concept of teaching. In the teacher-centered environment, the student can rise only to the level of the teacher—at least until the teacher gets out of the way! But people builders can enjoy watching individual students surpass even their own level of influence and leadership. Jesus had a glimpse of this when He said to His disciples, "'Anyone who has faith in me will do . . . even greater things than these'" (John 14:12).

Summary

When the *We Build People* vision comes to the teacher or individual leader, it requires two key areas of focus: the individual and discipleship. Teachers must think and teach toward the individual and toward discipleship in order to become people builders.

Once that transformation of thinking takes place, simple habits can be developed that provide the targets for each student. Efforts to include, instruct, involve, and invest people have great meaning in an environment where individual discipleship is the priority.

Ultimately it is the small-group influence of the teacher that makes building people happen. It's more than a vision for the local church. It's a way of life for those teachers who want to make an eternal difference—who want to build people!

Bibliography

Arn, Win and Charles. *The Master's Plan for Making Disciples.* Pasadena, Calif.: Church Growth Press, 1982.

Braden, Suzanne G. *The First Year.* Nashville: Discipleship Resources, 1987.

Callahan, Kennon L. *Twelve Keys To An Effective Church.* San Francisco: Harper and Row, 1983.

Colson, Charles. *The Body.* Dallas, Tex.: Word, 1992.

Damazio, Frank. *The Making of a Leader.* Portland, Oreg.: Bible Temple Publishing, 1988.

Eims, Leroy. *The Lost Art of Disciple Making.* Colorado Springs, Colo.: Navpress, 1978.

Finzel, Hans. *The Top Ten Mistakes Leaders Make.* Wheaton, Ill.: Victor Books, 1994.

Galloway, Dale E. *20/20 Vision: How To Create A Successful Church With Lay Pastors And Cell Groups.* Portland, Oreg.: Scott Publishing, 1986.

Gangel, Kenneth O. *Feeding and Leading.* Wheaton, Ill.: Victor, 1989.

Gorman, Julie A. *Community That Is Christian.* Wheaton, Ill.: Victor, 1993.

Greenleaf, Robert K. *Servant Leadership.* New York: Paulist Press, 1991.

Heck, Joel D. *New Member Assimilation.* St. Louis, Mo.: Concordia, 1988.

Hemphill, Ken. *The Antioch Effect.* Nashville: Broadman & Holman, 1994.

Hull, Bill. *Can We Save The Evangelical Church?* Grand Rapids: Fleming H. Revell, 1993.

_________. *The Disciple Making Church.* Old Tappen, N.J.: Revell, 1990.

__________. *The Disciple Making Pastor.* Old Tappen, N.J.: Revell, 1988.

__________. *Jesus Christ the Disciple Maker.* Old Tappen, N.J.: Revell, 1984.

Hunter, George G. III. *How To Reach Secular People.* Nashville: Abingdon, 1992.

Kraus, C. Norman. *The Authentic Witness.* Grand Rapids: Eerdmans, 1979.

Logan, Robert E. and Larry Short. *Mobilizing for Compassion.* Grand Rapids: Revell, 1994.

__________. *Beyond Church Growth.* Old Tappen, N.J.: Revell, 1989.

Martin, Glen and Gary McIntosh. *The Issachar Factor.* Nashville: Broadman & Holman, 1993.

__________. *Finding Them Keeping Them.* Nashville: Broadman, 1992.

Miller, Herb. *The Vital Congregation.* Nashville: Abingdon, 1990.

Murray, Sheila Bethel. *Making a Difference; 12 Qualities that Make You a Leader.* New York: Berkley Books, 1990.

Oswald, Roy M. and Speed B. Leas. *The Inviting Church.* Washington D.C.: Alban Institute, 1990.

Ott, E. Stangley. *The Vibrant Church.* Ventura, Calif.: Regal Books, 1989.

Peck, M. Scott. *The Different Drum.* New York: Simon and Schuster, 1987.

Rainer, Thom S. *Eating the Elephant.* Nashville: Broadman and Holman, 1994.

Ratz, Calvin, Frank Tillapaugh and Myron Augsburger. *Mastering Outreach & Evangelism.* Portland, Oreg.: Multnomah Press, 1990.

Richards, Lawrence O. and Gilbert R. Martin. *Lay Ministry.* Grand Rapids: Zondervan, 1981.

Sanders, Oswald J. *Spiritual Leadership.* Chicago, Ill.: Moody, 1980.

Spader, Dann and Gary Mayes. *Growing A Healthy Church.* Chicago, Ill.: Moody Press, 1991.

Stanley, Paul D. and J. Robert Clinton. *Connecting, The Mentoring Relationships You Need to Succeed in Life.* Colorado Springs, Colo.: NavPress, 1992.

Swindoll, Charles R. *Dropping Your Guard.* Waco, Tex.: Word, 1983.

Towns, Elmer. *Winning the Winnable.* Lynchburg, Va.: Church Growth Institute, 1989.

Westing, Harold J. *Create and Celebrate Your Church's Uniqueness.* Grand Rapids, Mich.: Kregel Publications, 1993.

Westing, Harold J. *Evaluate and Grow.* Wheaton, Ill.: Victor, 1984.

Wilkinson, Dr. Bruce. *The Seven Laws of the Learner.* Sisters, Oreg.: Multnomah Press, 1992.